WHAT
WE KNOW
SO FAR

WHAT WE KNOW SO FAR

Wisdom Among Women

COMPILED AND EDITED BY

BETH BENATOVICH

St. Martin's Griffin ◪ New York

Design by Sara Stemen

An Oracle Press Book

LIBRARY OF CONGRESS CATALOGING–IN–PUBLICATION DATA

What we know so far : wisdom among women / Beth Benatovich, editor.
   p. cm.
  ISBN 0-312-14759-7
  1. Middle-aged women—United States—Psychology. 2. Wisdom.
I. Benatovich, Beth.
HQ1059.5.U5W48   1995
305.24'4—dc20   95-20244
                                        CIP

10 9 8 7 6 5 4 3 2

For my daughters, Lynne Benatovich and Laurie Benatovich Vega

and for my husband, Mel Berenson
Thank you, yes!

Contents

Acknowledgments

I am immensely grateful to all of the women who agreed to be interviewed for this book, who opened their doors and their lives for the purpose of sharing their truth with us all and so have made this book possible. Your courage, discernment, generosity, and grace are a permanent inspiration to me.

I regret that I can offer no more than a heartfelt thank you to the many women who gave hours of their time in support of this project but who could not be included because of space limitations—your wisdom is also a part of the collaborative spirit of this book.

Thank you Abe Rothberg, Michael Harvey, Lisa Gillim, Sheila Markin, and Sandy Relin for endless cheerleading, loyalty, and love through all the years.

Special thanks to Mari Schatz, Michael Glaser, Susan Murante, Doris Blum, Tracy Donnelly, Mara Engle, Toby Miller, Diana Langston, and Lucy Molloy, who facilitated my efforts to make contact and appointments; to Al and Robert Olanoff, who helped a fledgling enterprise get started; and to Nancy Etheredge, artist and designer of kindness as well as talent.

Preface

A woman not quite old, certainly not yet wise, set out on a journey to seek the women of age, the wise women, to find out what they knew. Naked, stripped of all her preconceptions, she knocked on many doors. Could you tell me what it is to be an older woman in a world that values neither? she asked. Can you say what you have lost and won? Can you bestow your kindness and grace upon me, a stranger, and upon other women who, though strangers, might benefit from your wisdom?

And the women opened their doors, offered tea, offered coffee, offered little candies, and offered their intimate stories to a person they had never met and would probably never see again. With unthinking generosity they did this, as women often do. They told of mothers and fathers; of growing up female in the Depression, in wartime, in the world of the twenties, thirties, forties, and fifties; of education, yearning, passion; of menstruation, sex, lovers, husbands, and children; of aspiration, censorship, failure, achievement, mastery; of the loss of love and breasts and husbands and the mothering potential; of the search for self and the ultimate, triumphant finding; of sensing one's place in the universe, of order and dissolution and deaths, rebirths. In the telling, there were often tears, and almost always laughter—the kind of laughter that carries the seeds of freedom. The stranger walked away from each meeting with a sense of wonderment, admiration, and gratitude. And she went home and wrote the words down.

There was something midwifish about the process, she thought: the magical opening of doors, the generous gift, the evoking of something vividly, vitally alive. It reminded her of conversations with old, trusted friends, where it was taken for granted that the truth was the most important thing, that privacy was less important than intimacy, that what was uncovered would be of value, if not right now, then some other time. Wisdom, she reflected, has always been shared in this way among women. In kitchens, on porches, in backyards, over coffee cups, canasta cards, mah-jongg tiles, on the telephone, in church pews, at the hairdresser's, women have always told *each other* their stories, because who else was listening? The world? No, not lately. Their husbands? Sometimes; more often not. Lovers? No, not particularly. Children? No, youth is impatient with wisdom, particularly the wisdom of women, particularly their mothers. Friends? Yes, they have always relied on their friends, both as listeners and tellers, witnesses and trustees. In vital conversation with friends, their lives could be mined for the treasures just waiting to be unearthed, uncovered, and, possibly for the first time in their lives, esteemed. Archaeologists of the spirit, they told each other what it was to be a woman, to be *other,* to live on the periphery, to help and be a caretaker but never to be taken care of quite enough, especially when that caretaking function is over. To be a stranger . . .

Perhaps this is why the women of this book were willing to share their stories with another stranger, whom they must have recognized as alike, akin. Several times, she asked, "Why are you doing this?" And the answer was always, simply, To help.

To help, they said. To help other women locate the source of their own grace and power—the power to create, not exploit. To help share insight, in order to change prevailing prophecies about older women—that we will succumb, for instance, to cultural expectations of demoralization and decline, rather than integration and new growth. To help us commemorate the differences among us, so that we might be inspired by the similarities. To help bring the understanding of women to a world that needs it now more than ever, whether it recognizes it or not, whether it blesses it or not. To help us see with the clear, patient, intrepid eyes of wisdom; to help us invent another way of going forward, toward our common destination.

This is a book about insight and transformation—about women who have struggled and triumphed, who have *changed* in some deep and powerful way, who have *learned* something important about being a woman and a human being in twentieth-century America. A woman, Marion, said, "My soul was a blossom in bud for fifty years, until the light shone warm and it unfolded." Another, Anna, said, "I was afraid for sixty-two years, but then I forgot I had ever been afraid before." "I had to give up ignorance," said Lucille. "The one who dies with the most consciousness wins," said Gretchen. "A simple act of kindness can change the world," said Matilda. Janine, offering the antidote to passive grief, said, "Let us choose joy." In all their different ways, each woman reported, in words that connected their private experience to the history of many, about the capacity of wisdom to neutralize victimhood and fear, to release authenticity and freedom, the freedom to say, with an earned, fierce conviction: This is who I've become.

Here are the tales, as individual as fingerprints, as intimate as dreams, that women have always told. It is not the work of one writer, but a chorus of strong female voices—compassionate, furious, self-effacing, confident, ambivalent, sad, joyous, hauntingly beautiful—to augment the unheard voices of all women of wisdom, women who have lived life, faced death, and have something momentous to tell us. It is a song we have sung—together.

*"For wisdom cries out in the streets
and no man regards it."*
—WILLIAM SHAKESPEARE

WHAT
WE KNOW
SO FAR

PATHFINDER

∽ *Erica Jong, 52* ∾

Erica Jong's first book of fiction, Fear of Flying, *made her famous at the age of thirty-one, selling 10 million copies in twenty-seven languages. She grew up on the Upper West Side of New York City and graduated from Columbia University with a bachelor's and a master's degree in English literature. The best-selling author of five other books of fiction, seven books of poetry, and a just-published midlife memoir,* Fear of Fifty, *she lives with her husband, Ken Burrows, and her teenaged daughter, Molly, in Manhattan and Westport, Connecticut.*

My best friend and I were sitting in my apartment this morning, having breakfast in the mirrored dining room. My friend couldn't avoid looking in the mirror. She kept tugging and pulling at her face and saying, "Do you think I need a face-lift?" And I kept saying, "I don't know, do you think I need a face-lift?" Those mirrors were inescapable. Finally, I said, "Let's take down these goddamned mirrors, we've got to paint over these mirrors!"

I do worry sometimes about losing physical attractiveness. It's been a part of my life. It's given me a certain amount of power, though of the most ephemeral kind, and not the only kind I ever aspired to. I think it's a horrible trap for women to confuse being young and beautiful and charming with real power, which I define as authority, skill, influence. We must remember that it's a temporary power that we lose at thirty-five, anyway. But, since it's so difficult for most men to conceptualize women as anything other than daughters, or bimbos, it's hard to reach the stage when you stop being the adorable daughter in the miniskirt whom men want to take to bed. That's about the time you begin to understand that *you are where the buck stops.*

I was wonderful at being the adorable daughter in the miniskirt, very good at pleasing older men—the good daughter to my father and my grandfather, the good student to my male professors in college. I used flirtation to be charming and get attention. It was a role that was easy for me, but I saw it as fake. I understood that to be loved *only* for being a good daughter or a cute young thing was easy to get, but who wanted it? We all want to be loved for being ourselves, not just some reflection of a man, even someone we love. It's a temporary power, and I knew it, even while enjoying it for all it was worth.

In recent years, though I still sometimes play with the idea of getting a face-lift, I look at myself and see these character lines above my nose—my whole family has these furrows—and I think, "I'm growing into my face." I don't mind that it's not a girlish face, I'm proud to have earned all these stripes and wrinkles. Of course I want to look as attractive as I can, but what would I do with a twenty-year-old's face, or a twenty-year-old with mine? I know things that she doesn't know, can't know. And then I think back to how I was at twenty, and understand that for everything you lose, you gain about a million things.

I grew up in the fifties, when girls were expected to be *good*. I failed miserably at that. I always was a bad girl, in the best sense—assertive, and sexual, and outspoken, and saying *no* to people who wanted me to do this or that, or be this or that. But my pattern was always to alternate between periods of rebellion and periods of guilt—between being flagrantly bad, and then atoning by being gooder than good. I wasted an enormous amount of time worrying about approval—from parents, teachers, boyfriends, even from girlfriends—trying to change myself, to fit in, to please, even if it meant deforming my own needs. Of course it didn't work anyway, trying to please, because to be a woman in this society is to be eternally in the wrong. But it was time squandered, time I can never get back.

Women intellectuals were honored in my family. Everybody read and wrote—poetry, letters, journals. My father was a songwriter and a successful businessman, my mother, a gifted artist, with whom I've always had a very stormy relationship. She grew up in the feminism of the twenties and had a kind of bohemian ideal of womanhood, which she abandoned when she had three daughters. I was highly critical of her for that, resenting the mixture of messages I got from her. On the one hand, she was a bohemian artist who had worshiped Edna St. Vincent Millay in her youth. On the other hand, after she got married and had children, she always lived a very elegant and bourgeois life. I suppose I must have expected her, if she was a *real artist*, to go out into the world and fight to promote her own work, knock on doors, do whatever was necessary to become successful as an artist. Instead, she became the designer for my father's business, perhaps to save her marriage—I don't really know why. She and my father had and have a very close relationship, and maybe somehow she thought if she promoted her work the way she could have and should have and probably wanted to, her marriage would have come apart. But I was very busy trying to establish myself as a person separate from her, different from her. Like all mothers, she was very protective of her daughters. She wanted me to marry the kind of person *she* thought was right for me. Instead, I married, first, a poor guy who was a schizophrenic, second, a Chinese psychiatrist, third, a much younger man, who was at least a Red Diaper baby like me, who came from a Jewish and intellectual family. I kept doing the opposite of what she wanted, I think just to define myself. I wanted to show that I wasn't *her*.

In the last few years, my whole relationship to her has changed tremendously. The other night at dinner, I said to her, "You know, when I wrote this midlife memoir, I finally understood what you had done for me. You gave me the freedom to be imaginative." She said, "Oh, of course I did, I was like that myself. What's such a big deal?" She was a little embarrassed by my tenderness, because she's so used to fighting with me about everything. But she's eighty-three now, her heart is not as strong as it was, and I know I'm not going to have her forever. I feel, now, how precious she is to me.

I now know that I had to go through those marriages in order to find out who I was and who I wasn't. Each marriage was a kind of apprenticeship in which I learned something of importance. Until my later forties, I honestly believed, in a gut way, in what Colette Dowling called the "Cinderella Complex": that somewhere there was a man, better than the one I have, who had the power to transform my life. I never really fantasized a powerful male figure—a business mogul, a Donald Trump, an arbitrageur who could give me a lot of money; I fantasized a beautiful young man, a poet, a perfect soul mate who would carry me off to live with him in a villa in Italy and through his amazing sexual powers, or his ability to be very loving, would change everything in my life and make it good. That romantic dream of *rescue* is powerfully seductive to many women because it's so Oedipal—the fantasy of the all-powerful parents who will take care of you forever. The greatest freedom I have now is that I no longer believe that anyone else can save my life. I may fall in love again, I may not, but never again will I believe that someone has the power to change my life through love.

One radicalizing experience was having a baby. One of the most transforming things about giving birth is that, poised in the middle of this incredible wrestling match with the life force, you are immediately connected with the sources of life, but also with the sources of death. There's a line in an Edna O'Brien novel—"His little skull spoke to me of holocausts." You think, "It's up to me, and *only me*, not only to give this baby life but to protect her from death. If I don't feed her, she will starve; if I drop her on the floor, her little skull will be crushed." All women, even those with no children, are caretakers. When our relatives get older, even our *husband's* relatives, we're likely to be the person who takes care of them. Men are shielded *by women* from this primal work. So as a woman you become very aware of mortality, less in denial about it, and that's good, that's important. Because death will out, one way or another, and you finally realize you don't have forever to fuck around, to be trapped by your neuroses.

All the things you suffer from when you're younger—writer's block, fear of criticism, fear of failure—"Oh, I can't write that, people will hate me, I can't confront that, I can't say that publicly, they might misunderstand!"—become far less important by the age of fifty. By now, I have finally come to understand that whether people love me or hate me has nothing to do with me anyway, or with what I do; it has to do with *them* and their generosity or lack of generosity. Truly creative people don't compete with, but are inspired by, other talented people working alongside them. The viciously critical ones are usually people who've never achieved what they wanted to achieve, who are neurotic to the extent that they can't work. You reach a point in life where you realize that you might as well do what you need to do, because your being loved or not being loved is really a function of the people you encounter and not of yourself. That is an immensely liberating insight. In midlife, as your friends begin to die—and the numbers really accelerate when you hit fifty—you say, "Okay, it's now or never!"

I'm much less neurotic and compulsive than I was in my twenties and thirties. I used to write and rewrite and rewrite everything I did. When *Fear of Flying* came to me in galleys, I read all the dialogue into a tape recorder to make sure it sounded "real." If I had to speak in front of an audience, I would prepare too much, have everything written down. I worried a ridiculous amount about what to wear; my lack of confidence was always getting displaced onto the clothes I was wearing. If I was invited to a party, I would gulp down three glasses of wine, terrified that someone would see through my impersonation. Now, I can be anywhere, with the best-known people in the world, and assume that they want to talk to me, and that if they don't, they're dumb, because I'm an interesting person. And if I'm not interested in them, I excuse myself and go home early so I can finish the book I'm reading.

I've always had blocks. Every writer has blocks. I heard Stephen King, who publishes two books a year, talking on the radio about his blocks. I've never completely lost that punishing critical voice in my head that says, "Oh, people will hate me for this." I started out as a poet, and was categorized as "only a poet" for many years. Then I wrote *Fear of Flying*, which was a first book, so the deal was not really rich for me, but somehow it became part of the culture. When you have a success like that, other writers hate you everlastingly, because very few can even make a minimal living at writing. Before *Fear of Flying* found its audience, it was bitterly attacked by critics who were appalled by its revolutionary message. They acted as if the world were coming to an end. Perhaps they were right; the world *as they knew it* might have been coming to an end, because it marked or signified a change in the consciousness of women. But, coming of age, as I did, in the middle of the second wave of the feminist movement, I was shocked by the bitter criticism I received from some very smart women, who should have known better, who couldn't seem to see through the deliberate way they were being pitted against each other, split off from each other by patriarchal men. If we could reach out our hands and unite different groups of women, we would have long since won many points we are still struggling for—reproductive freedom, equal pay, child care. The number of feminists who attack other women is shocking! It seems to me that if women are going to change the world, they first have to change themselves and rise above that competitiveness, which we have been taught, and learn to be truly sisterly to each other.

I love mentoring younger women. My daughter's friends are always asking me, "When should I lose my virginity, and with whom?" And I say, "Well, whoever it is, make sure it's somebody who's very loving and caring, who really appreciates you and will really make love to you, rather than making you feel abused in some way. Make sure it's somebody who will have safe sex and care about your health, so you don't find out the next day after sleeping with him that he has three other girlfriends." I have also loved the role of mentoring younger women writers, reading and giving advice on some of their poems, or which agent to use, or going over the galley proofs of their books. I spend hours on the phone with these women, some of whom have become great friends, because it is an article of faith in my feminism that women have to support each other. Because it seems to me that what we're engaged in is a great experiment, which is rejecting our society's false definitions of ourselves. Rather than competing with ourselves and with other women, we're learning how to create new definitions of ourselves, which includes being sisterly and supportive of each other. We're figuring out a way to forge new paths for ourselves.

Henry Miller said somewhere, "What is a hero? Primarily one who has conquered his fears." We all have a million *nos* in our heads that prevent us from exploring our full creativity, because of fears instilled in us by our parents, or by the society we live in. You better not draw because you can't do it perfectly; you better not play basketball because you're not tall enough; you better not ice-skate because you're not Olympic material; you better not play the piano because you're not musical. Every time I catch myself saying, "Oh, no, you shouldn't try that," I think, "Yes, I *should*." I should explore everything that scares me, in order to move through those blocks. A hero is not someone who has no fears. Maybe he feels *more* fear than other people, and is therefore propelled forward, to confront them, to vanquish them. We all have fears. It just depends on how willing you are to let them dominate your life.

I had a ten-year period after my third divorce when I was a single parent, and I started out thinking, "Oh, no, this is too scary, I've got to get married again right away!" But after a while, I got into *enjoying* not being married. I loved that I didn't have to ask permission of anyone if I wanted to paint my bedroom green, if I wanted to date one man in the morning and another at night, if I wanted to work all night and sleep all day. But I also saw how much harder women's lives are than men's. Sometimes I look at the way men rise in the world—men who are writers, doctors, executives—and I see them surrounded by loving sycophants and secretaries or wives taking care of them, and I think if one of these men had to do what I did for ten years when I was a single parent, they'd *die*! They simply could not function! Whereas I had *nobody* to share some of the tough stuff of raising a child. I'm sorry, now, that I didn't have more children without worrying about a man in my life. I ended up supporting Molly anyway, and raising her anyway, and felt exhilarated by the challenge and proud of myself for doing it. Though painful and difficult, at times, I don't regret a minute of it. And, in freeing myself from the romantic dream of finding *another* man to come along and rescue me, I learned that no one can rescue me except myself.

I think I got it, thoroughly *got it*, in the last few years. I remarried at forty-seven, my fourth marriage, and though I didn't consciously expect to be rescued, there were still remnants, in my fantasy life, of that old romantic dream. There always are. In the beginning of this marriage, I started to see that whatever was going to work was going to work because *I* made it work, and *he* made it work, and because we both cared about not letting it fall into the toilet. My relationship with my husband now is a very powerful, close friendship. We understand each other very well; we agree that we both have work to do and other lives outside of each other, and that if we can't do what we both want and need to do, we'll resent each other so much that we'll start to hate each other. What good is that? It would destroy the relationship, maybe not directly, but covertly, and just as fatally. What I'm chiefly free of, now, is the idea that somebody, other than me, is going to change my life—not even my husband, whom I love and feel very close to. What is going to change my life is what I create, through my work, through making my soul more knowing, through meditation, through spiritual disciplines, through mindful existence. Through talking more lovingly and caringly to myself. Younger women often say to me, "Oh, you seem so calm! How did you get to this point?" And I say, "It's a long story." Sometimes it takes a lifetime to gain that kind of serenity and self-acceptance.

A seminal experience for me was being president of the Author's Guild. I never thought of myself as a political animal, but the position required me to take strong positions, unpopular positions, because publishers were banding into these giant conglomerates and crushing authors—taking away their electronic rights, their rights, in fact, to make a living from their work. The board was composed of a bunch of older men who were used to doing things the old way, who wanted to stay on the good side of publishers, be taken out to lunch, make nice— they were fooled by all that. These men were livid about my activism. My husband said, "I thought I married Virginia Woolf, but instead I married Mother Bloor!" What changed for me is that I understood that I wasn't going to be universally loved, because I was saying things that people didn't want to hear. I was rocking the boat, and people who rock the boat are not necessarily adored. That was a very important recognition. It happened in my late forties, and brought me to a point where I saw the inevitable. I said to myself, "You can't be other than who you are."

It's so liberating when you're finally able to jettison working for love and approval, to understand that you either have it, as a gift or a blessing, or you don't. My work has put me up against it all the time. Now, just when I have a new book coming out, I anticipate the onslaught. There's a lot of love out there, but there's also jealousy and hatred and negativity. The negativity, however, can no longer stop me from speaking out. I'm very religious, in a nonorganized religion sort of way, and believe that we're put on on this planet for a reason, that in working out our destinies and reaching other people, we're meant to influence other people's spirituality. By communicating the truth of ourselves, we are intersecting with other people's lives, inspiring them to be completely themselves, unneurotically, to be unafraid of revealing themselves, to use their full creativity. So I take as a general principle that my being in touch with my feelings, even the bad ones, helps other people to access their own and validate their own. I finally understand that what's valuable about me is that I'm a shit-disturber and a revolutionary, and that perhaps being criticized is an indication that I'm doing something *right*.

I believe that this is a moment of history in which we are engaged in a kind of spiritual revolution—the kind of revolution that creates pathfinders. As women age, we're put up against the materialism of the culture in a very cruel way that almost nobody else experiences. Ursula Le Guin wrote a wonderful essay in which she addressed the question of "What do we do when the species is through with us?" She suggests that as we enter the second half of our lives and are no longer in thrall to the species, we become, in a way, enthralled to the universe, because we have the wisdom that comes from all that birthing and separation and connection that goes on in the first half of our lives. So we're making new paths here. We're asking how we can make a contribution that is not simply a biological contribution. Nobody ever addressed this question before, since we've never had such an unprecedented longevity before. We're addressing it now, almost for the first time in history. Older women are again being accorded their ancient role as prophetesses and advisers, as they were in Native American societies and others throughout history. That's the great transformation that's happening again in our time. In looking to things other than the *body beautiful* for inspiration, we're being *forced* to redefine the second half of our lives, to become pathfinders. Rather than accepting the negativity of others, the lack of esteem, the invisibility, we are choosing to bravely engage the world, to confront injustice, to see the things that need to be changed in the world, and go out there fighting. This is a very courageous thing to do; we're doing it now, because we're choosing *not to throw ourselves away*.

THE ROSE

ᥫᦒ Eartha Kitt, 67 ᦒᥫ

As a dancer, actress, and nightclub singer, the legendary Eartha Kitt has appeared all over the world—France, Turkey, Greece, Egypt, New York, Hollywood, Las Vegas, England, Sweden. She was born on a farm in rural South Carolina "sometime around 1928"—lacking a birth certificate, she never learned her true age. While still in her teens, she joined the Katherine Dunham Dance Company; two years later, while touring in Paris, she performed in a solo cabaret act, which made her an international sensation at twenty. Still actively singing and performing, she is also the author of two memoirs, and currently lives alone in Pound Ridge, New York. She has one daughter, Kitt.

From the very beginning of my life, I was a reject. My skin was the wrong color: I was too black to be white, too white to be black. "Yellow gal," I was called. One of my earliest memories is of hiding under the house with the chickens, the cats, and the dogs, listening through the cracks of the floor to an argument my mother was having with the man she wanted to marry. "I won't have that yellow gal in the house," he said. I never found out who my father was, nor did I believe that the woman who said she was my mother actually gave birth to me. In any case, this woman gave me away when I was five years old to a family who made me feel far more unwanted than she ever did.

I have no sense of time—that may be partially what saved me—but it must have been a few years that I stayed with this new family. I was the work mule, the ugly duckling, a source of amusement and contempt to the other people in the house, again because of the color of my skin. It's hard enough to be discriminated against by white people, but even more painful when you encounter racism within your own race. I was the first one to get up in the morning, get the wood, make the fire, cook the breakfast—I was hardly tall enough to reach the top of the stove—then work in the fields all day. If there was enough food, I was fed once a day. If there wasn't, the animals got the table scraps. The two teenage children, Gracie and Willie, used me as a play toy in every form and fashion you could think of. They tied me to a tree and sexually abused me, then dared me to tell. Who could I tell? There was nowhere to go, except into the forest, which was my safety, my sanctuary. In the forest, I could live with my only friends. I could eat what the squirrels, the birds, and the rabbits ate—berries, seeds, plants, nut woods, surrounded by nature, birdsong, animals, I found the only happiness I knew as a child. But eventually I had to go back to the house, where I was constantly reminded of my difference, my strangeness. Since there was no safe place for me, I decided early that I'd have to create a place of my own. Since everyone around me was telling me that I was nothing, I had to find a way to make that nothing into *something*. If I was an ugly duckling, a reject, I had to find a way to turn all that *merde* and manure into a beautiful rose.

After my mother died, my aunt sent for me to come live with her in New York. My bedroom had no lock on the door, and every day when I came home from school, the man of the house was always there, drunk, thank God, most of the time, and always trying to put his hands on me. I remember the reek of his body, the constant smell of alcohol and rot on him. By this time, I was an athlete, having spent all those years running in the woods with the animals, so I managed to elude him and run downstairs, where there was a girl about my own age who also beat me up and called me "yellow gal." But at least she was better than the drunken would-be rapist upstairs.

Why, I wondered, did my aunt ask me to come to live with her? I always believed, though never confirmed, that she was my real mother. She and I resembled each other physically, both being tall and quite fair. I came to believe that she had this accidental pregnancy with me, then didn't want to be reminded of my dubious origins, so she gave me to her sister. But I was frightened by her vicious treatment of me. Once she threatened me with a piano stool that she was about to bring down on my head because I had gone to the movies instead of to my music lesson. If her boyfriend hadn't grabbed it out of her hands in time, I wouldn't be here talking to you now. At the High School for the Performing Arts, where I had won a scholarship, I learned how to cover my black eyes and bruises with makeup. My aunt cooked one meal a week, Sunday dinner, which was supposed to last all week. Usually about Wednesday, the leftovers ran out; sometimes I ate for the rest of the week, sometimes I didn't. For a time, we lived with her boyfriend in a one-bedroom apartment, where I slept on a couch in the living room. It shamed me that she was living with a man without marriage, so I called myself Kitty Charles, which was his last name. Every day it was brought home to me how dependent I was upon people who didn't really want me. I would get little jobs after school—shoe salesgirl, scrubbing toilets, sewing, anything to earn a few pennies on my own. Eventually, I ran away for good.

Once, my aunt sent the police to look for me. I had found a job in a factory, cleaning and mending the bloody uniforms of soldiers who were fighting in the war. The policeman told me I had until midnight that night to get back home. I thought, "Maybe when I get home, she'll hug me and tell me how much she missed me, since she went to all that trouble to find me." When she opened the door, she said, "Oh, there you are," and went back to bed. Not even a pat on the head. That *hurt*. I took a bath, washed my hair, changed my clothes, and left again for the last time. I stayed with my girlfriend Carmen, just a block away, went to school, and found work in another factory. But when the spring came, I jeopardized my job by spending all my time in Central Park, watching the tiny new buds on the trees and the birds and the formations of the clouds: This was the world of my spirit, the place of my safety.

Every time I have felt I was at the absolute end of my rope, something always happened. I believe that there is, inside every person, something that is unkillable. Somehow, although many people seemed to be trying to make me go away, I never went away, just kept on going. Before I could get fired from the factory, I met a woman who told me that the Katherine Dunham Dance Company was holding auditions for young dancers. What did I know about ballet? Not a damn thing, but that didn't stop me from running to all my friends, singing, "Babaloo ah yay! I'm going to join the ballet company and I'm never coming back! Babaloo ah yay!" I didn't know what the hell I was talking about. But for some reason, I was accepted at the company, and started touring across America and Europe. In Paris, somebody dared me to go out on my own, as a solo singer at a little Parisian nightclub. I took the dare, though absolutely scared to death! I had no act. In between songs, I stood there, frozen, mute, unable to say a word. But I said to myself, "I have to do this, I'm going to do this and will not be defeated by this fear." *Survival* was at stake, as it was in the forest of my childhood. And for some reason, it worked. The audience loved it, the critics loved it, and I felt I had survived, once again, something that could have killed me.

I've never felt that fear is my enemy. Fear is my friend. It offers me a chance to stay alert, keep growing, continue creating something new. If you don't take that sort of risk, you learn nothing. It's sad to see artists or performers repeating themselves over and over, fearing to venture out into new territory. I never do a song the same way twice. There has always been a part of me that was afraid to be seen, that had to be pushed out to meet people socially, strangers, but at this stage of life, I no longer want to be invisible. I think women in their sixties, seventies should be *more* out there, more visible, more committed to teaching what older women are all about. Sure it's frightening, but what other alternative is there? Every time I go out on the stage, it's hell, it's terrifying, I'm vomiting, I'm scared to death to cross that threshold between backstage and onstage. Quite often, my daughter has to push me out there. But once my foot has reached the other side of that threshhold, I forget everything except the artistry of giving my truth to other people. And once I hear the applause, it helps me to think, "Well, maybe you're not such an ugly duckling after all."

Before I ran away from home, I never really had a boyfriend. There was a Cuban boy I liked in high school, but I was afraid of him, afraid to show affection, afraid of rejection, afraid of sex. It was very difficult for me to go any further than having him hold me, since I was so uptight, holding in all the time. But when I did, eventually, fall in love, I fell hard. I didn't think of holding back, but simply gave myself fully, not thinking of consequences, getting hurt, or anything else. When you fall in love that way, and that love is returned, you're happy, you're safe. But if you're unlucky enough to have that kind of love rejected, there you are again, worthless, useless, unwanted.

I had one love of my life, and when that ended, I had to find a way to regain my own spirit. After quite a lot of emotional upheaval, crying, questioning myself, doubting myself, I was able, finally, to realize that it's a part of life, and love, and what you have to learn. I threw myself into my work. I went on. In the healing process, you discover that if you don't hide from suffering, don't try to cover it up, the work, your soul, becomes deeper and richer from whatever the experience is—even, maybe *especially*, if it's painful. You face it, you *live* it, and grow and mature from it. The temptation is always, of course, to sink into depression, into blame and self-doubt. I may have done that for about ten minutes or so, but then I said, "That's enough of that, let's get on with it." A few years later, I did get married, because I wanted a baby, but the minute I conceived, I unconsciously thought, "Okay, that's enough of this, you can go home now." Molly Bloom, in *Ulysses*, says, "What's the idea of making us this way, with a great big hole in the center of us, and men like rutting stallions?" That's how I felt with my husband— sexually incompatible. When the marriage ended, I had no desire to get married again. I didn't want a man to *pay me* to be his sexual plaything or his companion or his mate—that's a kind of legalized prostitution, isn't it? I still enjoy the company of men, still enjoy them as friends, but I don't think I want a man in my bed anymore. It was always so important to be independent, to never be in that horribly needy, helpless situation I was in as a child, where the people I was depending on were not *dependable*. We're taught to believe that we're just a half a person without a man, but that's completely untrue. I feel more like a complete person now, on my own, sharing myself with nature and it with me, than I did when I was constantly being pursued by men. And now, living alone feels right for me.

Being without a place of my own for so many years as a child, the idea of *home* has been very important. The best house I ever had was a converted stable, where I felt comfortable living among the spirits of the horses who had preceded me. Today, I live alone in a glass house—remind me not to throw any stones—with my dogs and my birds and the trees and the squirrels and the rabbits, just like that forest of my childhood. I'm looking at a bunch of pine trees standing outside my window. I trust that they are sensing my presence, just as I am sensing theirs. The grass on the lawn is turning brown because it hasn't been watered lately. I'm looking at the bird feeder and worrying that the squirrels will steal the birdseed. Recently, we had a series of violent thunderstorms here, and I was looking out at the wildness of the lightning and hearing the crashing of the thunder and thinking how beautiful nature is, even when it's dangerous. I felt safe in that storm, even though I knew it had the power to kill me, because the natural world has always taken care of me. So why should I be afraid of death, which is part of the natural process of life?

I believe in the concept of karma. I always tell my musicians, "Don't worry, God will take care of it"—not God in the sense of an organized religion, but in the sense of free will and choice. We all have a power within ourselves to choose to do good, rather than harm, to choose to help someone, rather than hurt, that says if you do wrong, that wrong is going to turn on you.

I'm not saying I've been an angel—I've done my bit of sin here and there. But I never consciously hurt anyone, or tried to exploit anyone for material gain. I never had much interest in material things, except to have a decent home, warm clothing, and the ability to eat three square meals a day. Even though I do sing those songs! Today, they call me the "original material girl," but that's absolutely not who I really am. Who I really am is Eartha Mae, the child of the forest, the urchin that nobody wanted.

As I grow older, I revert more and more toward my natural self. When I have to go out now, I warn my friends, "When you see me, don't expect me to look like Eartha Kitt." I don't have to look like a *Vogue* woman anymore. I'm more willing to be seen by others the way I see myself—Eartha Mae, just out of the fields. I like Eartha Kitt—she makes a nice living for me, she's funny and fun to be with. But she's not Eartha Mae, the child who suffered, who knows what pain is, the pain of being different. I understand, now, how gay people must feel, so rejected because they don't fit in. All of the misfits of the world are *me*. Once, in London, about to perform at a terribly la-di-da club, I heard some of the customers talking about me, saying, "She's so beautiful, what is she? Indonesian?" Then someone with an American accent said, "No, she's just a nigger." I went onstage with those words, the pain they caused me, ringing in my mind. All that unworthiness, that desire for invisibility, came back to me in a rush. The hurt as a child never goes away. The rejection never goes away. The worst feeling in the world is to be rejected because you're different. We must all respect, no, *embrace* our differences. We must try to remember what is of real, enduring value and then figure out a way to connect with it—nature, children, grandchildren, relationships. I have now reached a point where I know what matters, know what's valuable. I feel the enrichment of myself, and want to exercise it as well as I possibly can.

I give my age as sixty-seven, though it could be anywhere between sixty and seventy. Since the number is completely invisible, completely unknown, I act against the numbers. About fifteen years ago, a doctor told me, "Eartha, don't you know that at your age you're not supposed to be jogging ten miles a day?" The minute I left his office, my whole body started aching. I still run in the woods. You don't have to pay attention to these stupid-ass doctors who expect you to fall apart. That expectation alone can create the reality! Get physical! Go to the woods and pick up a stick. Climb a mountain and look at the sky. Clean something, cook something, lift weights, go as far as your body tells you you can go. Because after you fulfill yourself as a woman, you must start fulfilling yourself as a *person*—one thing does not, should not, exclude the other. After you have given birth to a child, and that child grows up, it's time to give birth to yourself.

The evolution of life dictates that life must deteriorate in order for something new to come alive. Everybody was complaining about the horrible winter this year, but I thought it was wonderful! My dogs and I were romping around in the snow and the ice, and to me it was absolutely gorgeous. There is a purpose in winter, just as there is a purpose in spring. We are only here to enable something else, someone else, to be here. The energy of *this* body is the fertilizer for succeeding generations. A table, a piece of wood, is made up of atoms, which can either be split, for the purpose of making atom bombs, or used as fertilizer, once its life cycle is over, to create something of beauty. I prefer to think of myself as fertilizer, as food for the living energy of others who will follow me—the kind of fertilizer that can grow a beautiful rose.

THE MORNING IS
WISER

⌁ Bel Kaufman, 84 ⌁

Bel Kaufman, author of the number-one best-seller Up the Down Staircase *and the novel* Love, Etc., *was born in Germany and brought up in Russia during the Bolshevik Revolution. At twelve, she immigrated to the United States, learned English "by osmosis," and later graduated magna cum laude from Hunter College (where she is in the Hall of Fame). She received an M.A. from Columbia University. The granddaughter of Sholom Aleichem, she has taught in New York City high schools, at City University of New York, and at the New School for Social Research. She is also widely in demand on the lecture circuit, speaking on such topics as: "Jewish Humor," "Don't Flunk the Teacher," "My Grandfather Sholom Aleichem," and "Survival Through Humor." She is the mother of two and the grandmother of one.*

When I was eighty, my friends gave me a birthday party. I danced the night away, had a marvelous time, and we all celebrated this landmark birthday. But the next year, when I turned eighty-one, I had a totally different feeling. Why did that one year make such a difference? I no longer felt, "Hey, I'm eighty, isn't that terrific?" but that I had entered *my eighties*—the last decade. And suddenly I bumped smack into the knowledge of my mortality, knowledge that was always there, but never in the forefront of my consciousness. That caused a dramatic change, not so much in my activities as in my ways of thinking as I went about my daily routine. I cleared up the mess on my desk, discarded some stuff, and started thinking about traveling lighter. My activities haven't changed much—I still do a lot of public speaking, writing, and much traveling. Every Thursday, I go dancing with a group of friends, and once a week, I go to a dance studio and dance with a professional. But now the thought—*the last decade*—is constantly with me, not morbidly but factually, reinforced by ever-more-frequent visits to friends in hospitals and to funerals, the losses of people dear to me. There was a funny cartoon in *The New Yorker* that showed a man reading *The New York Times* obituary page, with the little balloons coming out of his head saying, "Ten years younger than I, five years older than I, three years younger . . ." and so on. That's what I tend to do. There's the feeling of deprivation, of irreparable loss, and the sense of something ultimate. But always, always, there is the life-sustaining humor that has rescued me from despair so many times in my life.

Another change, now that I am *in my eighties*, is the liberation that comes from the decision and the ability to say *no*. Salesmen often call me on the telephone to sell me something. They say, "Hi, Bel? How you doing?" And I say firmly, "How'm I doing *what?*" Or sometimes I'm kinder, I'll say, "You've caught me at dinner. Give me your number and I'll call you while *you're* having dinner." At one time I would have been unable to say no even to that salesman. I was a rather diffident person in my twenties, thirties, forties. It never showed when I was teaching or giving a speech, because I always felt confident in the classroom and in front of large audiences. But in intimate situations—with mother, teacher, authority, husband, friend— my desire to please made it almost impossible for me ever to say no, for fear that maybe they wouldn't like me. Now, I say no without a trace of ambivalence. Nicely, but no. You notice how, even as we're talking, my back straightens, my shoulders go back, my posture improves? That's because, when you reach a certain age, you finally know your value.

I was twenty-two years old when I married the first boy who kissed me. In those days, if you went to bed with a boy, you had to get married. I thought, having no basis for comparison, that I was in love with him. I had just received my master's degree, and was offered all kinds of fellowships to work for a doctorate, but instead, making the sacrifices that so many women made, I saw him through medical school and internship by immediately taking a teaching job. It was a bad marriage, but I kept waiting: till the children grew up, till the children went to school, till the children went to college, balancing on that tightrope of trying to be the perfect wife and charming hostess, and sobbing in the bathroom at night. Finally, after twenty-nine years, I went to see a lawyer. The lawyer said, "You have no lover, you have no money (I had turned all my earnings from teaching and writing over to my husband), and you are leaving. Why?" It was then that I realized that it was not really a choice I was making. It was either live or die. I opted for life.

So, absolutely terrified, I left my husband and our fourteen-room duplex, found a one-and-a-half-room studio, and began writing my first book, *Up the Down Staircase*. I remember typing in that tiny room on a small manual Underwood and noticing that some of the funniest pages of that book were getting spoiled by blobs of my tears as they dropped onto the paper while I was typing. That's how frightened I was—a woman alone, at midlife, for the first time, who had always been the dutiful daughter, the good student, the patient, giving, forgiving wife—no longer mother, no longer wife. Who *was* I, really? And then to be suddenly there, in that tiny room, writing the funny book, with the tears falling on the pages—well, having lived through that, I knew I could endure anything.

People talk about the depressing and demoralizing period of the menopause, but I was hardly even aware of it. Nor did I ever have a problem with men rejecting me because I was not a nubile twenty. On the contrary, they seemed to respond to the intelligence, charm, and humor of a fiftyish woman. And it was liberating to find that I was much freer sexually, once released from the fear of getting pregnant. Of course, now there's a new fear, AIDS, but I'm speaking of a time before that. I never felt more free, as a sexual person, than after the age of fifty. I found myself not only attracted to men but being attractive to them, because I was able to enter into relationships without fear. Men respond to that. They sense that freedom, that juice, that readiness to take and to give pleasure, and are drawn to it. They don't count the rings on the tree trunk. In those postmenopausal years, despite the wrinkles, I found that I was a desirable person at a dinner table or at a party. And for the first time in my life, I was discovering who I really was.

Sholom Aleichem has a very funny line someplace: "A man may be likened to a carpenter. A man lives and lives, and then he dies. So does a carpenter." That's it. We all have to face reality: People live and people die. When we're young, we think death is perhaps possible; when we're older, it's probable;

but by the time we reach our eighties, it's inevitable. So now I call myself "an old woman," even though I don't, on most days, look old or feel old. I hate euphemisms like "the older woman." Older than *whom?* Older than *what?* I prefer the word *old*. It's an honorable word. So I say, as an "old woman," or "an elderly woman," my memory is not as sharp as it was. When I meet people whom I know, I often forget their names. That worries me more than a little pain here or there. At one time, I would have carried on a conversation and tried to guess from the context who they were. Today, I no longer pussyfoot around. I say, "Forgive me, I know we've met, but I don't remember your name. Please tell me." And they're not insulted, and they tell me, and I might make a joke about it: Did you hear the one about the two octogenarians? One says to the other, "Oh, I know you, but at my age, I don't remember names. What is your name?" The other one says, "Joe Smith. What's yours?" And the first one says, "How soon do you have to know?"

With age, one learns one's priorities. One dispenses with the trivial. One doesn't have time for everything and everybody, and becomes necessarily more discriminating, more selective. That clock is ticking louder and faster each day. Nineteen ninety-five? Impossible! It was just 1985, wasn't it? So I would say priorities shift. And if there has been a death or a serious illness, that's when the intensity of that shift in priorities takes center stage. My mother was always living in the past and regretting her errors. That's an enormous mistake—a human failing, but a mistake. We must *carpe diem*, seize the day, enjoy everything we can at this moment, because yesterday's gone and tomorrow's unsure. The preciousness of every ordinary moment is emphasized with every tick of the clock. Isn't it a magnificent day today? And after this terrible winter, what a pleasure just to inhale and exhale! One grows conscious of these small, ordinary pleasures in a way that youth isn't structured to understand.

I love the honesty that is possible at this age. Last week at a dinner party, I met an elderly man who stood up politely every time a woman entered the room. I said to him, "You were well brought up." He said, "No, I taught myself." I love that! Such honesty is not possible when we are younger. I don't play games anymore—either verbal, sexual, or social—games that I used to be quite adept at. I'm finally released from that terrible, terrible need to be liked and accepted by everybody.

The mind cannot grasp the idea of nothing. I believe that there is some energy or power—I don't mean a goddess in a turban or a god with a white beard—some vital energy in the human being that cannot become nothing. Whether it's a flower that springs up from the grave or a tree that lives from the ashes of a cremation, we are, all of us, valuable, thinking, feeling creatures, and it isn't only the pumping of the heart or the convolutions of the cerebellum that makes us what we are. It's only with the imminence of my own death that I'm beginning to think, "Well, there is a something, rather than a nothing." I can't prove it, of course, but now that I'm *in my eighties*, I sense the presence of things not visible to the naked eye.

I have a friend who is a sad sack, a pain in the neck to all her friends. She lost her husband years ago, and she keeps calling, wailing, "What can I do, what shall I do, I'm so *lonely!*" And I tell her, "You live near the Y, you were once interested in drawing, take a course in drawing. You once did this, do that." "I can't, I'm too old for that, I'm too tired for that, I'm so *lonely!*" Well, that is not the way to spend one's last years. They may not be golden, they may not even be brass, but there's some solid metal there.

Many more people than we know have various hidden talents. "Some mute inglorious Milton" lying in some churchyard . . . Why mute? Why inglorious? Because they never dared to write that poem. So that a woman who has always wanted, perhaps, to do ceramics, or some fancy knitting, or study Spanish or whatever, couldn't or didn't take the time for herself, because a woman is a nurturer, a woman gives, a woman feeds, a woman says, "There, there, baby, it'll be all right. . . ." She needs somebody to say that to her, too. A woman I know was interested in painting, but she didn't have much talent for it. In her house, she had a large, empty wall, so she began to hang some artists' paintings on that wall. That is how, by accident, she became an art dealer.

A character, Varya, in one of my books, gives a Russian proverb: "The morning is wiser than the evening." Whenever I'm discouraged or lonely or afraid, as I have been many times, I always try to remember that it will pass, everything passes, and I will feel better in the morning. Jewish humor is full of examples of survival through laughter, teaching us how to thumb our noses at adversity, to turn the tables on tragedy. Through Tevye, Sholom Aleichem says philosophically, "If you can't have chicken, a little herring will do. If you can't have herring, with God's help, you'll starve three times a day." And you're chuckling, but you don't starve. Or: Another of his characters, blind in one eye and myopic in the other, too poor to buy eyeglasses, wears only the frames without any lenses. Asked why, he says, "It's better than nothing." So: You can either say, "It's better than nothing," or "The morning is wiser," or, a phrase I find very comforting, "This, too, shall pass." One of the definitions of depression is lack of hope—you can't imagine that you're ever going to feel better. The novelist William Styron almost killed himself because of that. But if you just manage to stay alive, you will find that there will be a morning, and the morning is wiser.

Yesterday, I went to the funeral of one of my old friends. As we were leaving the funeral parlor, I said to my husband, "Somehow I can't imagine *my* children giving eulogies for me when I am dead." He said, "Don't worry, they will." And I said, "Oh, I hope to live to see that."

THE RETURN TO JOY

✌ *Janine Pommy Vega, 53* ✌

Janine Pommy Vega was a member of the Beat Generation and the author of nine books of poetry and two books of essays. She is a teacher and performance artist who has performed her work throughout North America, South America, and Europe. During the last eighteen years, she has been awarded over four hundred residencies as a teacher for the New York State Poets in the Schools Program, and has traveled extensively as a lecturer at universities and as a poetry workshop leader in prisons such as Sing Sing, Rikers Island, and Attica. She lives in Woodstock, New York.

D*ysfunctional* is too weak a word to describe the home that I came from. When I was growing up, my parents were passionately involved with each other, in a positive way, until I was about eleven or twelve. Then, all of a sudden, they had some kind of argument, she never forgave him, and that was that. However, the marriage lasted for another twenty-six years, until my father's death. They didn't talk, make love, or eat together for all that time. Although they both loved and accepted me completely, their disaffection from each other caused my relationship to them to become like a juggling act, in which I had to show both of them that I loved them, without alienating either parent. I didn't understand any of it. I only knew that there were great depths of things that were never communicated—the silence in that house was like a presence, it was so real and palpable.

I tried certain things to give me a sense of what it might be like to live in a real home. I redecorated my room to make it look like the kind you see in the movies. I painted it, put in a closet, a phone, hung pictures and paintings, and when it was all done, knew instantly that it was not what I was looking for. The external trappings of reality, of nice things in a nice room, gave me a feeling of total emptiness. Nothing in that room, or anywhere else I saw around me, was leading me to the real existence I sought, which even then I must have known could come only from within.

Soon after that, at sixteen, I left home. I was interested in poetry, so I went where the poets were: the Lower East Side of New York. My girlfriend, one of my schoolmates, and I went to the Cedar Bar, where we met Gregory Corso, who

later introduced us to Jack Kerouac, Allen Ginsberg, Irving
Rosenthal, Peter Orlovsky. . . . All of this was very romantic
to me, a young kid, wanting to be a poet myself, surrounded
by all these wonderful writers from whom one could learn so
much, but to whom one never showed one's work. The thing
about the Beat Generation was that the women were never
really honored in any way. Somehow, the revolutionary spirit
of the time did not include the women. Later, I coined the
phrase "the mop and the muse" to describe how the men used
to think of us. While we cooked, brought tea, cleaned up, and
so forth, the men wrote the poems. They did the real work,
the true work of poetry. The effect on me was that I had a lot
of trouble taking myself seriously, as someone who had my own
poems to write. I'd show them to my roommate, Elise Cowen,
and to Herbert Huncke, one of the older Beat writers, but I
never said that I was a writer, only that "I write a little." Then
I met someone who gave me the great gift of helping me to
own my own voice and give myself permission not only to
write poems but to be a poet.

Fernando, my husband, was a painter, a Peruvian, ten years
older than I, who always introduced me as "my wife, the poet."
When he was painting, I would bring him a cup of tea. When
I was writing, he would bring me tea. That taking for granted
that our work had equal value was the great gift I got in the
marriage, something that has lasted until this day. But it also
taught me that talent doesn't belong to me, to you, or to anyone
else who possesses it, but to all of us, and must be honored and
protected in the way one wants to take care of anything of
value.

Drugs were an important part of that culture. We were a
generation that was trying to lose ourselves, disappear, test our
boundaries and connect with some higher purpose in the universe. Though I didn't analyze it then, I now see that the using
of that amount of drugs may appear to be a way of enhancing

life, but actually *reduces* the vitality and intensity of the moment. It's impossible to communicate anything you've experienced while under the influence of drugs. Your mind, heart, and soul are muddled, rather than clarified. And, of course, the effort to disappear is doomed because of the narcissism of that whole drug-taking process.

I think in this life, there are very few ways in which a person can disappear, the way we tried to through drugs. One of them is your work. Another is through love. There's nature walking, and there's meditation. I can't think of any other ways. When we disappear, we're serving the universe best by our disappearance. For instance, when I'm working now, there's no ego there, there's no "me" there, there's no obstruction or shadow between me and what I'm doing. I'm a teacher and a writer, and always, *always*, the best teaching and writing gets done when "I" am out of the picture, and there's a profound focus on the other person or thing in this transaction—the student, the empty page. But it doesn't really matter what kind of work it is. You could be, say, the maître d' or maître dame at a fine hotel, and you're in charge of seven waiters and reorganize the floor and make things run efficiently and comfortably—that, also, could be the work, the way to disappear, to best serve the world. Eventually, if we don't die first, we come to a time in life when there is just no more time to get high.

At this age, I've been feeling more and more that there's no time to lose. No time for small details, for trivial pursuits, for haranguing myself, as I did for so many years, making the kind of judgments about myself—whether I'm important enough, smart enough, lucky enough, happy enough, thin enough—that took up so much of my attention for so long. It's actually a kind of arrogance to judge yourself, even when you're comparing yourself *unfavorably* to others. There's arrogance in judging yourself either *better* or *worse* than everybody else. I'm always telling my students that we have to get rid of our self-importance when we're writing, or even when we're just living. The assumption of self-importance has to do with youth. It creates self-consciousness, a state that is paralyzing for any creative person. But the longer you live, and the more work you do, the easier it is to see that *in the service you shine.* By ourselves, there's really not that much that is worthy of notice.

There's a Hindu sage who says, "To identify yourself with the body is a worse sin than killing a thousand cows." In youth, I was outgoing, outer-directed, and sexually and emotionally adventurous. Today, I no longer feel that I have to run out and find myself a man or be with somebody else or look outside for what I need. If someone comes along, that's fine, but no longer necessary. It's a real freedom not to be driven by hormones. And although I know that I am a getting-older woman, my chins are dropping, my bones are weakening, I certainly don't look as good as I used to, all that means nothing now, because a long time ago I stopped identifying myself with my body. In the last couple of years, the work that I'm doing, both as teacher and writer, has grown more intense, and the focus is much stronger. When I'm approaching A, these days, I find there is no B or C. It's a kind of letting go of everything that isn't *it*. That kind of focus takes an enormous amount of energy, but it's energy I'm glad to give. I work, come home, sleep, get up, focus, work. I'm constantly *on* it, after a lifetime, it seems, of distractions and irrelevancies.

My husband eventually died of a drug overdose, which made me a widow at twenty-four. I thought that was it, my life was over. For many years, I felt this sort of unbearable freedom, this unassuageable grief at losing this man who I was so connected to. We didn't have any children, and I knew I could go anywhere and do anything I wanted to. I traveled to Peru, met another man, and very quickly thought I was in love again. But soon I came to understand that I was superimposing my desire for what I wanted onto the face of somebody else. I had to leave for several months to come back home, and when I saw him again, I didn't recognize his face! It wasn't the face I had been carrying with me, the face I thought I was in love with. It was only a reflection of my own desire to be in love again, a search for that lost joy.

I remember when I was a kid, I had a boundless joy, just a powerful sense of how great a gift it was to be allowed to live on this earth. Then, when my husband died, I seemed to lose it, that original sense of deep joy. I guess I must have attributed the state of joy to being married, to being in love, being involved, accompanied. I worried: Wasn't I ever going to get married again? So I started climbing mountains, journeying to distant places, looking for that source of joy. And now I'm so glad I didn't find it in the mountains, in the cities, because it forced me to find it within, which is where it all started in the first place.

About fifteen years ago, I traveled to Bolivia to a place called the Island of the Sun, which was a small island in the middle of Lake Titicaca. One moonlit night, I was walking up and down the shore of the lake, sensing the presence of the sublime within all that devastating beauty, something central there, some answer to my question. It was about the time I realized that the angel I was looking for in "the other" was never going to be found in the outside world, but must be sought within. So I told myself, "If what you want is within, well, let's get down to it, let's find it." I rented a little house in one of the island's three tiny villages and spent a year and a half living as a hermit. And in that state of extreme isolation, where the people spoke no Spanish or English, where there was no one who knew me, and not a living soul to talk to, you can't help but learn certain things. The most important thing you learn is that you can die out here, that you're all alone, really all alone in this world. There's nobody who's going to save you, to ride in at the last minute and save you from yourself.

And that knowledge, once you really *get it*, can free you from those longings to be rescued, to be taken care of by a powerful male figure, or the wish to be released from your responsibility to yourself.

Only the ripest apple falls from the branch. When it is the right moment to fall into the love of yourself, you have to be ready; you have to have experienced things—losses, deaths. So a primary focus for older people has got to be a return to the joy within. We have come to expect that in age, we will find a diminishment—that we will get less and less and less of what we need. In later life, we find ourselves in a dead-end alley. We see there's nowhere to go, nowhere to turn. But we forget that there is a trapdoor in the alley, one that leads down to our own souls. Yes! There's nowhere to go, no escape, that's the great opportunity that later life gives. We have no choice but to locate our inner source of strength, because there's nobody out there who's going to give it to us. We're therefore *forced* to go to the place that it all started in the beginning, the source of our deep joy, the joy we felt in childhood.

In the Hindu tradition, you are first the child, then the householder, then the forest dweller. The Hindus figure that after the age of sixty, you have earned the right to go out into the forest and truly seek God without any distraction, any interruption. So when you pass forty-five, fifty, a kind of winnowing begins to take place, a throwing away of what the soul doesn't really need, and a clearer vision of what's important. You finally feel that you are in the right place at the right time.

I was in a head-on collision about thirteen years ago. At the same time, I was involved in an intense love affair. I didn't know how it had come about, but all I knew was that I was in the wrong place at the wrong time. So I went looking for the goddess of healing, to England, Ireland, and France. I started out at Westminster Abbey—that bastion of male dominance and imperialism, sexism, classism—which just choked me. But later, after visiting Ireland and France, I was invited to go back to Westminster to give a reading. I read my poems in the Poet's Corner, and those feelings of being in the wrong place at the wrong time just dissipated. The Spanish poet Juan Ramón Jiménez wrote:

> I have a feeling that my boat
> has struck, down there in the depths,
> against a great thing.
> And nothing
> happened . . .

It may seem that nothing happened, but in fact something powerful *had* happened. And that enabled me to be standing there in the old place in a new way.

We are always putting obstacles in our own paths. Women, particularly, do this. Wanting to deaden the pain of my husband's death, I was carrying this big umbrella around. Under this umbrella, I would never see anything—the sun, the light, the dark—and nothing could hurt me. The umbrella in that case was drugs, but there were many other times I placed unnecessary obstacles in my own way. When I was much younger, I was fascinated by music but never studied it. Instead, I had a long series of love affairs with musicians, idealizing and supporting the male's role, as a substitute for doing it myself. Then I learned from a terrific male poet in St. Louis how much of an enhancement music can be in a poetry reading—how, when used as a backbeat for the words, the words have more accessibility and vitality. My poet friend introduced me to a musician who taught me how to relax into it, rather than tightening and fighting it and feeling that I wasn't really a player, but a speaker, a solo speaker. So getting past that obstacle was strengthening; it gave me another tool to reach more people with more effectiveness in my work.

It's no big secret that for thousands of years, there's been a getting away from the natural home that we're born into, the earth, and a headlong plunge into the mental and the intellectual—into technology and heartless problem solving. The capacity of the brain and the mind is beautiful, but when it gets divorced from its roots, then it becomes destructive—the kind of force that wants to make bombs and destroy its enemies. The power of the mind can become authoritarian and punishing when we divorce ourselves from the female side of nature.

The one who suffers the most is the force that is most ignored: the earth, the women who lose their husbands and children, and the children who lose their fathers. The earth is suffering from being maimed by those who appropriate its riches for their own profit. Children suffer from the lack of fathers, from the neglect and disrespect for their own uniqueness. And women, who have been the life-givers, suffer because they have almost forgotten how to honor that power in themselves.

I remember the end of my mother's life, when she went through hell, just pure hell. After her children left home, she felt that she had ceased serving the ongoing civilization, her function was over, her inner wisdom a meaningless commodity. No one was asking her what she knew. She became one of those old women at whom people laughed at the Grand Union: "Uh-oh, here comes that little old lady with the hat again." Her will was the strongest of any person I ever knew. She just closed in her circle, smaller and smaller and smaller, until she was talking to the TV, and finally, at the end, willed herself to die. My father had a certain amount of power, which enabled him to create a life for himself, social connections, friends. My mother also had power, but she never knew it, never even recognized it in herself. So that power, unused, unacknowledged, fell in on her, and she died an embittered and angry old woman.

We must all reclaim our power. An old woman who has

gone through love, childbearing, loss of love, divorce, widow-hood, loss of the mothering potential—this old woman has an incredible power. We all have it, we were born with it, it is our birthright. When we discard and ignore women after their time of procreation is over, we commit a terrible crime against the earth, which is just as ignored and abused whenever she has no particular monetary value. The earth is a giver and a mother, and mothering, as we all know, is heroic. We must honor everybody who does as she does—who bears fruit, as she does, who nurtures and takes care, as she does, who knows what we all know on some deep level but don't pay sufficient attention to. The state we're in right now—sex is death, food is poison, the water is no good, the air is ruined—is the consequence of cutting ourselves off from our deepest roots. The ego-driven, vertical power structure has brought us to the brink of extinction. But power is not vertical; it's horizontal; we're all sharing it. Women are shorn of their power and their grace every day, because they have forgotten the power within, the original joy. We have to reestablish our connection to the old ways. We have to look in the right place. We can either choose sadness, constriction, despair, or we can choose joy. Let us choose joy.

EVERYONE'S AN
ATHLETE

❧ *Billie Jean King, 51* ❧

Billie Jean King's efforts on behalf of women's tennis have made her one of the most famous and best-loved players ever to play the sport. The holder of a record twenty Wimbledon titles, she was ranked number one in the world five times, and in the top ten in the world for seventeen years. She is the author of five books on tennis, the founder of the Women's Tennis Association, the Women's Sports Foundation, and the cofounder of WORLD TEAMTENNIS, an organization that is dedicated to creating equality of opportunity for girls and boys. Billie Jean is a member of the International Tennis Hall of Fame and the National Women's Hall of Fame, and, in 1990, she was named one of the "100 Most Important Americans of the 20th Century" by Life *magazine.*

Everything we learn in sports can be applied to life. Great athletes have to learn how to be *in the moment*—to forget that last point they threw away, some stupid mistake they made, a double fault, whatever. Human beings have to learn to stay focused in the moment, too, not dwell on the mistakes of the past or the wishes and hopes of the future, neither of which—past or future—really exists. Athletes learn to notice what just happened in the moment, to avert a bad habit, or repeat whatever it was they did right. And being in the moment as people, we notice things, our senses are sharpened, and that noticing makes us feel our connection to everything and everybody else *out there*. Our minds and our bodies are one. The body always tells us when something is right or something is wrong. We know in our heads, our hearts, or our stomachs. We just don't always know how to listen.

I have been learning throughout life to listen more and more to my body. I used to live too much in my *head*, rationalize too much, make large intellectual commitments, while ignoring my gut reaction to the situation. So my gut is going, "Bing, bing, bing, hello?" but I'm too busy *analyzing* to listen. Now, when I feel my gut getting tight as a knot, or when I hear that "bing, bing, bing," I say, "Stop! My gut is telling me something, let's figure out a way to use that information."

My parents always say I was born intense. I had my first tennis lesson at the age of eleven with Clyde Walker, a teacher who was giving free group lessons at a public park in Long Beach, California. That was the day I knew I wanted to be the number-one player in the world. I couldn't wait to tell my mother. I ran out of the park and into the car, where she was waiting to pick me up. I remember everything so clearly about that day—the blue sky, the smell of the eucalyptus trees, the squeak of the springs of our green DeSoto Fluid Drive as I was jumping up and down yelling with excitement, telling my mother how much I loved playing tennis: "It's so great, Mom, I get to run, I get to hit a ball, it's like dancing, Mom, I'm going to be a great tennis player someday, Mom, hurry, let's run home and tell Daddy and Randy!" She said, "That's nice, dear, but you better make sure your homework's done." She figured it would probably last two weeks. My father thought it would be good for my health, so he said, "Great! You just keep it up." But neither of them bargained for my passion, which just grew and grew and, really, never stopped growing, even to this day.

My father was a fireman, my mother a homemaker. Before I reached the age of eleven, I was encouraged, or at least allowed, to do anything I wanted. I loved to play touch football, to run, to jump, leap into the air, catch the ball, play and have fun. But around the age of eleven, my mother wouldn't allow me to play football anymore—she wanted me to be a "lady." It was like putting a knife in my heart. What did that mean, to be a lady? That I couldn't go out and play, couldn't have fun anymore, had to be "feminine," which meant someone other than myself? It made me absolutely miserable. Like almost every other female athlete I have ever known, I never fit into the mold of being a proper lady, and, as a result, I felt like a complete misfit when I was growing up. It wasn't only my parents, it was my peers, it was models held out to me, it was in the schools and magazines and newspapers and television *every single day*. My friends could never understand why I only wanted to play tennis all the time. "Why aren't you coming to the slumber party?" they'd ask. But I felt different, and that was both good—I was already working toward my goal of being the best tennis player in the world, number one—and bad—I wasn't like the others, most of whom didn't know what they wanted to do yet.

Today, young girls are encouraged to become professional athletes, primarily, though, in individual sports—gymnastics, figure skating, tennis, golf—where they're the sweet little star, who looks good, with all the attention paid to them alone. It's very narcissistic to be a top athlete. Your whole day is spent focused on yourself. You get up in the morning and you eat right. Then you go and work out. Then you do whatever your sport is, then get a massage, have a healthy dinner, and go to sleep early so you can be in top form in the morning. Reporters want to interview you, everyone caters to you, you look great, you're in the best shape of your life. But once they get out in the real world, these athletes have no other frame of reference. In the workforce, in the office, even in the family, they're at a huge disadvantage. Larry King, my former husband, and I had a dream to create WORLD TEAMTENNIS, where this disadvantage could be turned into an opportunity. There are two boys and two girls on every team, so that everyone has a chance to contribute equally to the outcome of the match. We emphasize doubles more than singles, and teamwork with supportive and leadership roles. Girls need to learn how to be team players, how to get along with others and work toward furthering the goals of the larger group, not just their own.

Girls are also not encouraged to be active within their bodies. Too often girls, unlike boys, feel uncomfortable in their own skins. They are urged to excel in educational areas, but so often when it comes to the physical realm—sports, dancing, running, walking—they're just not *in* it. They prematurely resign. Physical activities are another way to know ourselves, especially as we get older. Mature women who are active in their bodies are much happier emotionally, tend to have better health, less osteoporosis, fewer of those physical debilitations we have to face as we age. Some of the senior tennis women in their seventies, eighties, even into their nineties—every one of them has her weight down, body fat down, they look vibrant; they are my inspiration. That's how I want to be when I reach eighty.

I married young, like all good girls of my generation, at the age of twenty-one, way before I had time to find out who I was, or anything about my truth, my sexuality, my spirit. It was very hard for me to find out these things *after* I was married, because it caused pain to people I loved. We always think it's going to be safer to find a Prince Charming and get married, which I think is just hysterical! Not only is it not fair, either to the man or to yourself, it's not even *reasonable* to expect someone else to take care of you forever and ever. We all have to learn how to care for ourselves, married or not.

With only one important exception, I do not know a single woman athlete who does not have a strong fear of being considered "unfeminine." The only exception is Martina. She has always known who she was, ever since she was three years old. I said, "What? How did you know then?" She said, "I always knew, I never had any interest in guys." That wasn't true for me. From the age of fourteen until my marriage, I always had boyfriends, I was always interested in the male sex. Now, I don't know whether I'm lesbian or bisexual, and labels of that kind don't really interest me. I like men and I like women, and that's the way I am. And I've grown more interested, since I've gotten older, in being who I am.

There's something about passing the age of fifty that makes us all begin to think of making a change, a good change, something toward more spiritual depth. I remember Barbra Streisand being interviewed on television and sort of guessing in advance what she was going to say. I guessed that she would talk about simplifying, divesting herself of material possessions, and there she was, talking about selling her huge collection of antiques and some of her houses. She talked about slowing down, taking time to listen to her own inner voice. Like almost every other fifty-year-old woman I know, I'm concentrating on slowing everything down, trying to get more clarity. I'm trying to think slower, speak slower, so I can figure out what I'm feeling and what I want to express. And I've rediscovered physical fitness, in a way that fits my life now.

I've always had enormous energy, passion, motivation, drive. But these days, my intensity has gotten softer, gentler, calmer, nicer, slower. I like that, the reduced intensity. When I was playing professional tennis, I had only two overriding goals: to win matches and to create opportunities for women in business and sports. I was forced to take care of myself physically, watch my weight, eat carefully, exercise, and so forth. All that went completely out the window when I stopped playing competitively. I gained weight, pretty much gave up all physical training, and had to face up to all kinds of buried food issues that I think were expressions of my badly neglected spiritual side. With therapy, and a regular regime of meditation, I'm beginning to learn how to calm down, simplify, get rid of material things, sell some properties, narrow my focus in one way, and expand it in another—which means create more time for me.

I feel more balanced, more true to myself, and many times stronger, emotionally. More truthful. I think what I tried to do—and failed, since it's not really possible—was to separate my mind and body, in order to play competitively and win. The rule we were always taught in sports was the cycle of "stress, recovery"—you go out and kill yourself, then calm down, kill yourself and calm down again. I always had to discipline myself to go to the gymnasium, do the aerobic exercises, the weights, the treadmill, the bike, running—I *had* to do all that, it was part of the deal. So I wanted to get away from it. There's a book I like, John Douillard's *Mind, Body and Sport*, that encompasses a new way of looking at sports, and has renewed my interest in physical fitness. It's a much slower, gentler way of staying in shape, involving TM, modified vegetarianism, relaxation exercises, and biofeedback. I think this could be the future for everyone, because everyone is basically an athlete. Just walking is being an athlete, just breathing is being an athlete. This kind of slow, calm way of approaching sports is perfect for older people. Now I'm doing the treadmill, the bike, playing tennis, lifting weights again, going much, much slower—I've rediscovered the original *fun* I used to have when doing physical activities.

Quality of life can and should be absolutely wonderful at any age. It's true that all women of any age are discounted, older women most of all. But one of the great things about being invisible is that *finally* we can do anything we want, with no one watching over our shoulders. And that equates to freedom. As we age, we suddenly confront new choices, realizing that we have the power to become a much more positive force in life, sharing with people, choosing our friends according to who *we* like or love, because no one's noticing. To anyone who doesn't *see* me, I say, "Fine, you guys don't want to say hello? I'm not here? Well, great! Since you don't see me, that means I can have more fun than ever!" Instead of feeling depressed about being discounted, let's use it as an advantage and the solution to our problems in later life. Let's realize, accept, and fulfill our freedom. And when we do that, guess what? Everybody starts to notice. Pretty soon, when mature women finally do something wonderful with our freedom, the world is going to sit up and take notice. But that can't happen until we feel good about our freedom, instead of missing and longing for all those things that, when we're younger, make us unfree.

When I was five years old, I remember, I was helping my mother dry the dishes, when I had the most powerful sort of *flash*, a sudden realization about my future. I said to my mother, "You know, Mom, I'm going to have a great life. I'm going to do something *really special.*" Now I feel I'm not so unique, or any more unique than anybody else. Everybody is special, absolutely unique, absolutely a treasure chest. Of course, we have to open the treasure chest to find what's in there, we have to listen to our gut, our intuition, and be dedicated to our own truth. If we're going to be discounted and not be as beautiful, well, that's our first taste of freedom, maybe for the first time in our whole lives. Go and be whatever you want to be. Get into the moment, into the *now.* To be scared is normal, to be not scared is stupid. But fear makes you lose the moment, putting you into some kind of nonexistent future, what might happen. If we go *with* the fear, instead of against it, crossing that line into action, we find an exhilarating new world. Everyone's an athlete. Don't think about what might happen in some nonexistent future. Stay with the now, stay in the moment, like a champion. Sometimes it's a bigger risk *not* to do something than to *do* it.

THE THINGS
THEMSELVES

∽ *Lucille Clifton, 59* ∾

Lucille Clifton is the distinguished and acclaimed author of nine books of poetry, a memoir, and more than twenty books of fiction and poetry for children. Twice nominated for the Pulitzer Prize in Poetry, and the recipient of the Juniper Prize for Poetry, an Emmy, and two NEA fellowships, she teaches every fall term at Columbia University, and in the spring at St. Mary's College of Maryland, where she is Distinguished Professor of Humanities. Widowed for ten years, she is the mother of four daughters and two sons and the grandmother of five.

to my last period

well girl, goodbye,
after thirty-eight years.
thirty-eight years and you
never arrived
splendid in your red dress
without trouble for me
somewhere, somehow.

now it is done,
and i feel just like
the grandmothers who,
after the hussy has gone,
sit holding her photograph
and sighing, wasn't she
beautiful? wasn't she beautiful?

—Lucille Clifton

I had a challenging childhood. In addition to being extremely poor, there was a period of sexual abuse by my father when I was ten and eleven. It lasted only for a couple of years, but I felt that there was no safety for me in my parents' house, and therefore none anywhere. I once wrote a poem that included a line that represented myself as a child: "the small imploding girl." Always a reader, I turned into myself, and learned to trust nothing but the evidence of my own eyes and ears. This meant that I had to define my world in my own way, rather than buy other people's definitions of what was true, what was false, what was good, what was bad. And this knowledge has stood me in good stead all through my life.

Learning is process, not an arrival. You have to keep on doing it all the time. The poet's, and the full human being's, way of perception is to attempt to see things whole, in all their wonderful and terrible possibilities. Recognizing, for instance, that nice people can do terrible things, and a murderer can be kind to his mother. What I recognize in myself is the possibility for good, but also the capacity for unspeakable evil—as I once said in a poem, "to love the human—the silences, the terrible noise, the stink of it." In wanting to do good, we may do evil by *mistake*, unless we first recognize that there exists this possibility in all of us.

Being human is not easy. We need to work on it all the time. The fact that I had to learn early that there was no safety anywhere had the net effect of forcing me to pay close attention to what was out there in the world. It got me into the excellent habit of *seeing* what I look at and *hearing* what I listen to. It sounds funny coming from a writer, but you have to be careful not to get misled by words. Words are only approximations of what is meant, not the things themselves.

In our culture, the truth gets lost amid a barrage of words. We say so many things that are not so. We say we value children, and yet there could not be so many of them in poverty if that were so. We say we value art, yet most artists are ignored in America, unless they've won a Nobel Prize. We say we value wisdom, but I don't believe we do, unless that wisdom has something to do with making money or starting a corporation, and unless it comes from the mouths of men. But older people's wisdom is totally overlooked, and I think that is unfortunate. One of my poems contains the line: "America, history is chasing you like a mean dog." Any dog will keep chasing you if he knows you are afraid. The only remedy is to turn around to face the dog. The poem ends: "Old people understand this. They know how mean that dog is, and they know it's your dog."

Faulkner asked the question: "If the truth is one thing to me and another to you, how will we know which is really true?" Then he answers: "The heart already knows." We all know intuitively when we're being stupid, arrogant, sorry for ourselves, unkind, but we don't trust our own intuition, our own heart. We hardly recognize that we have an inner life. We substitute that recognition with belief systems and dogmas and even religions that are imposed from outside, mistaking the symbol for the thing, the form for the substance. I think that is a very bad mistake.

My mother was a poet who was once asked to collect her poems together in a book for publication, but my father didn't want his wife to be a public person. During those years, the forties and fifties, men always told women what to do, and women didn't know that they could say *no* to the men they loved. I wrote about how she burned her poems in the coal stove, "jewels into jewels." I started writing poetry while I was still in my teens, and never stopped, even through my years of young motherhood, when I had four babies in diapers at once. Nothing could stop me from writing. I think I must have persevered in such a determined way because I saw someone who was stopped, and knew what it cost her. How strange that it took us so long to strike the word *obey* from the wedding ceremony, to draw the line, to keep on being a person even after we got married.

When I was younger, I used to believe all kinds of goofy things. I used to think I was so smart. I tended to believe that if I was a good girl, all kinds of remarkable things would happen to me. I believed that the government would never lie, and that to be intellectually smart was important. Now I know that intellectual brilliance has a lower place on the hierarchy of importance than intuition and feeling, because intellect doesn't translate across cultures and across race and across the world, but feeling does. I may not think the way a New Zealander does, but I fear in the way she does, I'm angry in the same way, joy and grief happen inside us the same way. Placing more value on feeling than on mere logic and reason helps us to see people, not as "other," but as *akin* to us in some important way. And once we start seeing other cultures and races as not different but alike, not "them" but "us," the result is compassion—the opposite of hatred. Schools don't teach a child how to intuit, how to feel. Radio, television, the movies, the media give us a false view of the world. All these things make it difficult to become, and remain, a whole person. It's only as you get older, sometimes, if you're lucky, that you notice: These things have been misleading me. And you begin to count your own experience as valuable, and count your own understanding and attentiveness as valuable.

Sometimes other people don't bring the same level of attentiveness to me that I bring to them, and sometimes that makes me sad, or angry, as the case may be. For instance, I've been widowed for ten years, and have noticed that other people, particularly men of my age, do not always notice my human characteristics but are quick to pin a label on me: poet, for example, or professor. Sexually and romantically, they are interested in women of my daughter's age. It hurts my feelings. It puts me into a slot, and I go uneasily into slots of any kind. I wrote a poem about it called "do not send me out among strangers":

> this big woman
> carries much sweetness
> in the folds of her flesh . . .
> who will hold her,

who will find her beautiful
if you do not?

Menopause was difficult for me. I had a phase when I experienced a kind of nostalgia, thinking how great it was to be a mother and knowing that possibility no longer existed. I wondered why I wasn't more relieved when my periods ended, since I had suffered terribly from menstruation and called myself the "queen of clots." It affected my professional life, even my ability to travel. But after menopause, I felt that I was leaving a wonderful country, a country that I knew and loved, where I had many children and enjoyed nurturing them all, and entering a new territory, strange and unknown, the land of trying to figure out how to nurture myself.

As women, we're all so conditioned to take care of others that we feel guilty when there's no one around to take care of. One of the hardest lessons I ever had to learn was that I couldn't protect my children from their own lives. I still, once in a while, think I'll give it a try, but then I have to force myself to accept that these children of mine are almost middle-aged people now. When my daughter got divorced, I had to fight my tendency to get involved too much. Actually, I wanted to go out and shoot the guy, but I figured my ending up in jail wouldn't help her much. I tell myself that they have lives to live, and those lives will be like mine, with mistakes in them. I hope that they will learn the lessons that I see are there, but they may not do even that. All people, even one's own children, come with baggage. When they're little, you have to help them carry it. But when they grow up, you have to do that difficult thing of setting *their* baggage down and taking up your own again.

Everything has a price. For everything you gain, you must give something up. Lately I've been asking myself, "What did I give up for poetry?" and even, "Was the price worth it?" For me, I had to give up ignorance. And in asking, "Was it the right choice?'' I know the inevitable answer: Yes, it was right, because it got me to what I know now.

I've always been a spiritual person, though not a particularly religious one, to the extent that I've always been aware of two worlds: what we can sense with our senses and what we cannot. I've always known that there is another unseen, mysterious world, a world that is just as alive as you and me, but lately, in the last ten years or so, I am able to trust it more, and to rely on it more than on my intellectual process. When my husband died, I wrote that in his dying he was finally able to see "not just the shapes of things, but the things themselves." There is a hidden mystery in life, a sense of order, a sense of holiness that evokes in me a sense of wonder. Many people call it God. I call it the Divine. Once we recognize that the earth is a living thing, whether we can *see* the energy in an animate object or not, we begin to treat it better, realizing that there are some offenses we do not commit against other living beings. The poet Richard Shelton was addressing this subject when he said, "We will be known as the ones who murdered the earth." One of the exercises I give my students is to walk around, and everything they see, *everything* they see, they have to say, "How very odd." That skews their habitual ways of thinking, which I think is very good. We need to get out of these habits of secondhand seeing and see for ourselves, and not just the shapes of things, but the things themselves.

AN INTEREST
IN THE WORLD

ᑫᕼ *Grace Paley, 71* ᕼᑫ

*Grace Paley—acclaimed short story writer, poet, teacher, community activist,
and environmentalist—was born in the Bronx, the youngest daughter of
Ukrainian-born immigrant parents. She entered New York's Hunter College
at the age of fifteen and later attended New York University, but she left
before obtaining a degree. Until her mid-thirties, she wrote only poetry, then
she began writing short stories. When asked why she never published a novel,
she replied, "Because life is too short and art is too long." Of her six books
of short stories, the most recent is* The Collected Stories, *published in 1994.
She is the mother of a son, Dan, and a daughter, Nora, and lives with her
second husband, Robert Nichols, in rural Vermont.*

In every immigrant family there is always an aunt who never married—the tragedy of the family. Also in immigrant families, you often hear about the value of a good education. So while your parents are telling you that the most important thing is to get a profession, they are simultaneously pointing a finger at the aunt.

I grew up in the Bronx, the youngest daughter of Russian immigrants, who would have supported me in anything I wanted to do. The problem was, I only knew what I *didn't* want to do—go to school, for instance. I gave my parents a lot of trouble about that. Boys were important. Very, very, very, *very* important. I was always falling in love in high school. I joined lots of organizations to protest the Spanish Civil War and the Italian fascist invasion of Ethiopia. My youth was spent worrying about the condition of the world and falling in love, trying not to go to school, and reading and writing a lot of poems. Everybody was getting married then, during the war. My parents, who had hoped I would go to college and become something, *anything*, were somewhat relieved when I got married at nineteen. Once the children were born, they forgot altogether what a flop I was.

As a young teenager, I had the normal teenage attitude toward my parents: I felt that they were just totally stupid. They were both remarkable people—socialists, but very conservative in their socialism, it seemed to me. They were puritanical, too, about social and sexual matters. It seemed so ignorant to me. So I had normal but furious feelings about them, and gave them a lot of trouble because of not going to school and liking boys and stuff like that. But I always had the fondest regard for them.

I was sad to give them trouble like that, but I knew I couldn't help it and had no intention of changing. After my marriage, they stopped worrying about me, which made it possible to appreciate them again. By the time I was in my mid-twenties, I saw that they were pretty smart after all.

I've always loved the dailiness of marriage—the way being married is like other people's lives. Much of my life has not been like other people's lives, so I like that, the normalcy. There's something about getting to know at least one other person, the specialness of living together every day, that I like very much. Two things I tell my students who want to be writers are: First, keep a low overhead. Then, never fall in love, or even live together as a roommate, with someone who doesn't respect your aspirations. I wrote only poetry until my thirties, when I started writing stories. My husband—I always still think of him as a boy—encouraged me to keep on writing. Since I never got a degree, I never got *jobs*, really. I had forty different places I worked—most of them doing typing, steno, office work, office temping. . . . Sometimes it was for organizations that I worked for eventually, like tenants organizing. When our two kids were very young, we were supers for our apartment building, so we didn't have to worry about the rent. I did a lot of stuff for the PTA, because education interested me totally in that period—still does. I think the smartest people in the world should become high school teachers instead of professors. My son is a teacher on the Lower East Side. His students are Chinese, Dominican, Haitian, Puerto Rican, Taiwanese. Young people in their twenties who love the world a little bit should think about people in their twelves.

Whenever I've fallen in love, it's always been for a very long time. My husband and I had two children together and stayed married for twenty-four years. Now I'm married to somebody else for twenty-two years. The hardest thing I ever did in my life was to leave my husband. It went so much against my view of how to live, like making extra sadness in the world. I knew that it would be hell doing it. I knew that I would suffer as much as he did. But it had to be done. I'm friends with my first husband now—I like him a whole lot, and see in him now the boy he always was, the boy I liked so much. And getting to know two people, two men like that, has been very important in my life. You can't get to know somebody in that deep, daily way if you live with him for only a year or two, because most things are learned slowly: You have to put in the time, to live through things, to learn.

Now I'm learning how to live in a totally different place. I was a very city kid all my life, but five years ago, my husband and I moved permanently to a rural community in Vermont where we'd been vacationing for twenty years. Up here in Vermont, I feel related to this earth. Living here in the summer and winter has been very useful in my understanding of my connection with the weather, the ground, the growing of food. Rural people are up to their ears with problems about septics and trash disposal, which brings you closer to those decisions about how to handle the waste of our wasteful lives. The water that comes in here comes from someplace; now I know where that place is. There's a river about a quarter mile away where we swam for years, until most of last year. Then all of a sudden somebody put up a sign that it was polluted. The experience of being here, working in the garden, has helped me cement certain feelings I've always had about the meaning of life. For me, the meaning of life is the next generation. The meaning of life is the child. The meaning of life is the seedling: a tree seed, a flower seed. It holds true for everything that is alive on this earth. Not just me. Not just "us." It exists in terms of the absolute connection, among us all, among all the seedlings and all the children. I consider our child seeds as much a part of nature as a wolf's pup or a maple seed.

I'm a very "one day at a time" person. Where I am at any

given moment is where I am. When I look back at myself from a span of years, I know that the person I'm looking back at didn't have the capacity to look forward at herself in later life. The person I was in my twenties didn't know much, couldn't know what was going to happen. I had certain hopes. I hoped that I would have children and would always live with someone I loved. Somehow I thought about where this country would be in twenty years, or where New York would be in twenty years, more than about what I would personally be doing twenty years from then. Without knowing or realizing that I would become a writer, I just hoped that I would be able to keep on writing. However, being who I was, I guessed that probably I would not write so much, because of my own habits—delaying, getting distracted by the world. So I knew, once I began writing the kinds of stories I wrote, that I would have to do them the hard way, fighting my own habits and character. I was so easily pulled away at all times, from everything. If I was writing, I felt the tug of wanting to be with my family. When my kids were little, during the Vietnam War, I'd be pulled away from them to go to long, long meetings, lasting all day. Yesterday I spent the whole day with my new little grandbaby, when I was supposed to be working on my next book. But that's exactly how I want to live my life, and how I've always managed to live. It's not that I didn't worry about myself. I just sort of assumed I would be all right, without thinking grandiosely that I'd be wonderful, or as lucky as I have been.

I'm thinking of the things I still am that I always was— kind of disorganized, and putting things off for next week that I should have done last month. Right now, I'm compiling a new book of essays and reading certain things that depress me. Looking through my papers from twenty, thirty years ago, I see a letter I wrote in 1964: "I promise from now on I will answer all your letters. . . . I'm really organizing myself this year." Finding that letter was really depressing to me, because I found out that thirty years later, I am just where I was then. I have a kind of general surprise that I ever managed to get anything done. On the other hand, later life does present you with new opportunities—to learn something new, to grow in some unexpected way.

For instance, I find that I am able to speak up much more since I've gotten older. I used to get absolutely terrified speaking in any public arena, even, once, at religious services. I always told myself that if I didn't say something, I would be ashamed forever. So I would just have to force myself to stop trembling, and grab someone's hand and just *speak up*. That, I think, is what courage consists of: the knowledge that you'll regret it forever and be ashamed for the rest of your life if you don't say what's on your mind. Years ago, if somebody made an anti-Semitic remark at the dinner table, I might have let it go. Today, my tendency is to say immediately, "You can't talk like that. It offends me." Why? Because maybe I don't give a crap anymore. To hell with you if you're so ignorant. At the same time, having taught so long, I have this horrible teachingness in me. One of the things that happens in later life is you really know what's happened in the world. You're related to history. And you have an obligation to say how things were. So if I'm going to have a confrontation, I should be at least teaching someone something. There is that feeling, that obligation, that comes with age—the feeling that we'd better do some teaching *fast*, or else. It's a terrible thing for us old people to think that we might be leaving the world worse than we found it.

The struggles around and within the women's movement are of abiding interest to me. I've been endlessly concerned and interested and proud—*proud* is a funny word, since I had nothing to do with it—glad to have lived through this time. When I travel, I talk as much as I can to young women. Many women in the movement are always saying, "We don't have to worry

about the men, it's more important to worry about ourselves."
But we *do* have to worry about the men, because they're the
ones who are in charge of the world. Americans are the biggest
arms traders in the world, and getting bigger, according to last
week's *Times*. How we can think that selling guns to other
nations so that people can start shooting each other *over there* is
unrelated to the arms trade inside our cities, unrelated to the
persistent masculine view of how life should be lived—this is
heartrending to me.

Sometimes I try to talk about this with my husband, but
he refuses to discuss it, even though he agrees with me totally.
It's hard for men to accept the fact that it isn't *women* slaughtering
each other in Rwanda, Yugoslavia, Somalia, New York City,
Los Angeles, it's *men* slaughtering men and women and children.
It's like an enormous *blindness* that comes over people, as if
they've poked little arrows in their eyeballs or something. I can
see the pain and shame in the eyes of men I know, men of
good intent, hearing the news on the radio about three or four
rapes and murders in the last few minutes, but they won't talk
about it. It just makes them feel too sad. Of course most men
are not like that at all, and a great many young men have been
helped by the woman's movement to take a big load of macho
off their backs, a load that the rest of the world is trying to put
on. As women, we have a big obligation toward these guys.
We must see to it that little boys are raised in decency and
humanity. Many women are afraid that their boys will not be
men if they raise their sons that way, but I keep saying to them,
"Look, he's got balls, he'll be a man, don't worry about it! Your
job is to make sure he's a *good* man. He's got the equipment to
be a man, you've got the equipment to make him good."

I have never noticed one case where teaching humanity to
a boy made him less of a man. Not that we should feel bad if
a son decides he's a homosexual. Within the peace movement,

I met many young boys who were pacifists; a lot of them were the sons of army people. It's the *fathers* who frighten their sons away from masculinity, not the mothers.

Once I gave a talk to Harvard students. I said, "Brains are getting a very bad name. Because the brain is being used for *destruction* instead of *construction*. Pretty soon, with the survival of the fittest, the fittest person will not be the smartest person at all, but selected on the basis of not-so-braininess, so they'll do less harm. We don't want brains to get a bad name, so you guys—*start thinking!*" The brain can be used for good, too, so we'd better start educating our kids right from the beginning. If we last.

I always laugh when I hear people say they're fifty and they're finished. Maybe there's an expectation in America that past fifty, work will end, love will end, life will end, but in my experience, the opposite was true. Probably the most intense and surprising and exciting part of my life was in my late forties and fifties. You reach a point of some sense of what you can do in the world. You're freer than ever—free to do all kinds of work, free of the kinds of "couple" relationships where you had to go to those terrible even-numbered parties that were always two, four, six, or eight, but never five or seven. It's nice to be free of that, and free to find each other, too. Among my friends, some of their best relationships were made after fifty. I have been lucky to be involved in a lot of political work at a time when politics, particularly the women's movement, belonged to us all, so I was energized from the *outside*. If you're interested in what's happening in the world outside, interested in your neighbor, that interest is returned to you many times over.

Sometimes, I have moments when I'm afraid. If I stop to look around me, I think: I'm seventy-one years old and feeling fine, but my friends are beginning to get very, very sick, and some of them who are only a little older than me are beginning to lose their minds with Alzheimer's. It would be stupid not to be afraid a little, but we must all learn to live with fear. It's as if we were traveling to another country. Old age is another country, a place of strangeness, sometimes, and dislocation. There's a lot to be done in this country, and a great deal of pleasure there. There are friends, some of whom are sick and needful of you, as you will be of them someday. The world itself is very beautiful. It's a place where you have a lot to do. But you have to do it knowing that sometimes you will be afraid of this new country. I wrote two or three poems called "Fear." "Waking in the morning: Fear." You have to accept it, that's all. Pretend that you're in any situation where it was the first thing you did, like the first year you went to camp. So you went to camp and it was strange there, another country, but you lived through it and learned something. It's there, so why not call it by its name? Fear. And at the same time saying it's all interesting. Then you just live with it. It helps to think of your children and their children, who are counting on you to help out. It's not just yourself, it's the people in front of you and in back of you.

I hate the word *menopausal*. I don't mind saying "after menopause," but "menopausal" is too narrow. It suggests that all women after a certain age are alike. While it's insulting to suggest that all women become any one thing after menopause or any other time in life, many older gray-haired women go to meetings or panels, and unless you're known, you're treated as if you've just gone somewhere and are not *there*. It comes with gray hair, I think. If you're fortunate, and you have work to do, and are interested in the world, and you can laugh a little, then you realize that the people who think we're invisible, *they* are the dumb schmucks. That's why we all have to stick together, as women—for those of us who can be seen, and those of us who can't be seen.

THE CAGE OF SHAME

୧⊚ *Janice Mirikitani, 54* ⊚୨

Janice Mirikitani is a third-generation Japanese-American who as an infant was sent with her family to an internment camp in Rohwer, Arkansas, during World War II. She grew up on a farm in rural California, then graduated with honors from UCLA and with a teaching credential from UC Berkeley. A published poet, editor, community activist, and administrator, she has been the program director at Glide Memorial Church since 1978, creating recovery, women's, arts, and outreach programs for the poor and homeless of San Francisco. She is married to the Reverend Cecil Williams and has one daughter, Tianne.

Shedding Silence

She unknots her scarves,
the shawls,
the quilted squares . . .

This loosening of garments,
tearing of thread,
uncovering each layer

revealing her bare skin,
her lips
shedding

shedding
the silence.

—Janice Mirikitani

The older I get, the more elusive the quality of wisdom seems. My way of acquiring knowledge is to just sort of stumble into things, learning whatever I know almost by accident. Wisdom has become, for me, the willingness to struggle with my deepest fears and, as often as I can, to open myself to change. I must admit that I don't always enter my days with that determination. I have to be pushed, or push myself.

I was brought up on a farm outside Petaluma, in a rural setting that was isolated from the nearest community. That physical isolation was compounded by social isolation; all the neighboring farms were owned by my cousins and uncles. I was the oldest girl in the complex—six years old. For eleven years of my childhood, from the age of six until I left home at seventeen, I was sexually abused by a number of adult males in my family. The abuse ranged from incest to sexual torture and violent beatings. I was forced to witness the torture of animals: My main perpetrator would insert objects into the genitals of animals and watch them die. He would wring the necks of chickens. Have you ever heard a dying animal scream? A kitten, a puppy tortured? They writhe. It's beyond hissing, beyond screaming, beyond pain. You don't have to tell a child, "I can kill you, I can wring your neck, I can break you in half, I can do whatever I want with you. . . ." The child already knows she is nothing. She knows their power over her is absolute.

My mother was physically absent most of the time, and in extreme denial during the rare times when she was home. My grandmother knew, but she was helpless against the males in the family. She spoke very little English and I spoke no Japanese, but I could tell by her actions, her tears, and her tenderness toward me that she knew and yet loved me anyway. She would tell me, in her broken English, that there were people in the world who had to be evil, and others who were placed on earth for something better. She said, "What you must do is survive. You must live long enough to leave." My grandmother was my rock and my salvation, the only source of unconditional love I ever knew as a child. Without her, I'm sure I would have committed suicide, as so many violated children do.

For many years, I made excuses for all these men. They were Japanese-Americans who had been interned in the camps during the Second World War. Their pride and dignity had also been stripped away, and therefore they had to assert their power some way, even if it was only over a child. But none of the excuses I made for them helped *me*. The longer I renounced my anguish, my rage, the more powerless I felt, the more unworthy of being allowed to live. I started to feel that they were justified, that I must have done something to deserve it. I said, "Oh, I get it, *I* am the ugly one, the useless one, the stupid one. *They* are the creatures of power. I must be deformed, otherwise why are these people doing this to me?" And so, finally, I got the message that I was nothing, nothing at all.

For almost twenty-five years, I hugged this secret to myself, refusing to acknowledge what had actually happened. Of course on some level I *knew*, but did as much denying as was humanly possible without losing my sanity, my point of contact with reality. As a child, I had survived by reading fairy tales, dreaming, daydreaming, creating my own scenarios of escape and power and beauty. In my dreaming, I was Snow White, I was the Fairy Queen, I was Sleeping Beauty, who would sleep a hundred years and wake up someplace else. In the classic pattern of the incestuous system, I kept my mouth shut, reasoning that if no one ever knew, I could be a person like other people. Or at least I could imitate how normal human beings behaved, in the hope that I could become human myself.

When I left home, at seventeen, to go to college, I became the stereotype of the overachieving Asian student. My mother wanted me to go medical school, not because she believed I could become a doctor, but because I could then be around *guys* who would be doctors, thus acquiring power by proxy. I never made it past the first semester of chemistry. Instead, I switched to English literature and did bad imitations of good poets—T. S. Eliot, Dylan Thomas, e.e. cummings, Theodore Roethke. At UCLA in 1960, all the coeds were white, buxom, blue-eyed Marilyn Monroe look-alikes, so I went through college trying to be white. I was convinced that I had to marry and have a child by a white man. I longed for a child with white blood running through her veins, the hated yellow blood diluted. I needed to be needed; maybe a child could fill the emptiness within my soul. And, since white males *were* the power structure, the only gift I could give my child was the white blood which alone represented power in the world.

To find my prince, I dated a lot of frogs—abusive, possessive, oppressive white men who I "fell in love" with, all the while telling myself that however badly I was treated, it was probably my own fault. The more a man hit me, the more responsibility I took for it. The more possessive he was, the more it meant he "loved" me. I seduced as many men as I possibly could, taking pleasure not only in the power of being sexually desirable but also in my ability to steal these guys from their wives and girlfriends. I formed a lot of superficial friendships based on physicality, social status, and the profession of the boys we dated—doctors, lawyers—while simultaneously trying to join the middle class by overachieving in school. In short, I was a mess.

After graduation, I moved to Berkeley and started teaching school. Surprisingly, I loved the kids I was teaching—mostly inner-city kids, black kids. The ones in pain were my mirror. I was still seeing a bunch of men, not knowing what the hell I wanted. After a couple of years, I married an associate English professor at Berkeley—the symbol of a good father, who had the power of whiteness, the power and the ability to allow me to bear a white child, which I did. He was a good man and a very good father to our daughter, but unfortunately, I had married him for all the wrong reasons. And because I was still such a mess, the marriage ended after four years.

There are people in this world whose being, whose spirits are groping toward healing. I would choose friends who saw through me, whose pain mirrored my own. One of them suggested therapy, which was the very very beginning of my healing process, starting before I got married. But the relevance of therapy didn't become clear to me until years later, until my thirties. When I left home, I said, "That's it, it's over. I don't want to go back or *look* back, ever." I have enormous, almost unlimited stamina to run *away*. But the faster I ran away from myself, the harder I ran *smack* into myself. Sometimes I think that if it hadn't been for my daughter, I might have run right off the edge of the earth.

We go through each day making the decision either to live or to die. By requiring me to be responsible, my daughter forced me to decide *to live*. She was a great source of amusement and pride and a love that—here it is—a love I had never experienced with another human being before. It was the kind of love that had no power complex in it, no ulterior motives, nothing manipulative, nothing to gain. That was a huge change for me. When we divorced, she was four years old. Then I was a single mother for the next eight years. I was lonely as hell. I developed an addiction to alcohol, continued testing my attractiveness through countless sexual relationships, and covering my rage and shame with layers upon layers of denial.

From the time I hit twenty-eight until I was about forty, the thought of getting older, of losing the only power I had, was like a kind of death. The only power I ever knew was my youth and so-called exoticism, my body and my sexual desirability—what people call, with good reason, the "power of the pussy." Many women believe that the only thing of value we have lies between our legs. At least, I thought, I was good for something. Now I had to face again my fear that I might be good for nothing. So the fear of aging really began to slap me around. I was working with younger people, and that really hurt my ego. If anyone guessed my age right, I would get depressed for months. *Months.* Dreading every birthday, terrified of having to admit my age, mourning the loss of youth—I did all that. To be completely honest with you, I'm still not crazy about being the age I am. I would still love to have the skin, the stamina, the memory, and the body of a twenty-five year-old. But what I do know is that change is not only possible but *inevitable.* I always felt like a very *small* person, with very little to give. I do have something to give now, though I never really figured out what it was until I was almost fifty years old.

The eight years after my divorce were years of incredible busyness for me. The middle sixties was a radical time—antiwar protests, race riots, the ethnic-studies strikes in San Francisco—and all these political movements helped me come to terms with my *yellowness.* By this time, I had gone back to school for my master's and was working at Glide Memorial Church, itself a highly radical environment. Communities of all colors began creating coalitions to protest racism. That's when I met dozens of women who expressed their feelings of worthlessness, ugliness, emptiness, and invisibility because of the color of their skin. Absolutely *gorgeous* women were saying, "I'm ugly because I'm black or yellow or red, and I'm not thin like Twiggy, not blond like Marilyn Monroe." That's when I became, proudly, an Asian-American, a *yellow woman,* for the first time in my life.

We created three anthologies of prose and poetry written by Hispanics, blacks, Asians, Native Americans, all people of color, both genders. I began writing again, not overwrought Dylan Thomas poems about moons caught in trees, but about the internment camps, my mother's silence, American geishas, Hiroshima. The backlash to becoming yellow was to become antiwhite. I even became a member of the Red Guard for about five minutes—wore Chairman Mao buttons on my hat, carried the Little Red Book, being extremely loud and strident about my yellowness. I see now that it was just as much an identity question as it was when I was trying to be white. Who are you, who are you? was the question I was constantly raising with myself. But I was running too fast to find out.

All this time, I carried the shame of my childhood like a tiny ball of fire within me. I covered it up with sex, with food, with alcohol . . . masked it with makeup and tight clothes . . . wrote angry poems about racism, capitalism, injustices of all kinds, but never a single poem about the incest that had happened to me as a child. That all changed when, as Program director at Glide, I helped create a recovery group for crack-cocaine addicts. My attitude going in was arrogance: I am not like these people. I don't smoke crack, I am college-educated, a former teacher, I'm not homeless, not on welfare. I put myself on a little pedestal, immune, apart. The women in the group confronted me: "Who do you think you are, sex bitch!" they yelled at me. And still I sat apart, thinking I was better off, in better shape than they were. Then one day, I was sitting in the circle and listening to the women talking about being abused by their fathers, by a priest, being gang-banged by their brothers. One woman talked about lying very still while she was being molested by one of her mother's boyfriends so her baby sister wouldn't wake up and attract his attention. I sat in the circle and suddenly the being inside of me, the tiny pearl inside the oyster, the little ball of rage just burst open. I fell apart. The pain went through me. I thought I would die of it, so much pain, buried for so long. But the release of the pain started me on the road to transformation, a road I'm still on and will probably be to the end of my life.

Change is not easy for most people. Often a bad reality is preferable to the idea of change; we prefer to embrace the demons we know than the positive force we don't know. What I do know for a *fact* is that there can be no healing without pain, no transformation without truth. As much as I try to deny it or evade it, or to make it a little easier by justifying, explaining, excusing, I know inevitably it's just going to have to hurt.

Cecil and I were married in 1981, when I was forty. We had been close friends for sixteen years before our marriage. It was the first time I had ever had a close male friend, a relationship that was not based on mutual exploitation. We midwifed each other through some difficult times. He made me take a critical look at the patterns I had fallen into, and kept saying that

authenticity, honesty, emotional and intellectual integrity—
these were the things that counted. And because he was so
honest with himself, I was able to be honest with him, if not
yet publicly, openly. But right after that experience with the
cocaine recovery group, Cecil spoke in church about the children of incest. He asked if anyone in the congregation wanted
to stand up and talk about it. Ten or fifteen people got up to
tell their stories. I was blown away by their audacity, their
bravery; I thought, "My God, that's the same damned thing
I'm feeling!" Everyone in the room was transformed. At that
moment, I understood that every time we tell the truth, we are
engaged in a spiritual act. Because in that act of liberation and
affirmation, we contribute to somebody else's freedom.

The following week, Cecil asked me, "Would you mind
if I said in church that I am the husband of an incest victim?"
That really threw me. I asked, "Would it help if I told my
story?" "It would," he said. Ever since that day when I sat in
the circle and faced my truth, I was unable to manage anything.
I would fly off the handle at the tiniest provocation, fly into a
rage. But after I spoke out in church—it only took five minutes
to say it—I felt free.

For most of my life, I have been an atheist, an anti-God
person. As a child long ago, I used to sit in the sanctuary of
that small-town church waiting for someone to pick me up,
and pray to God for hours and hours—pray for the abuse to
stop, for the torture to stop. But it never stopped. So I gave up
on God. I figured that either he didn't hear me, didn't see me,
or worse, didn't care. Then I came to believe that he didn't
exist at all. In talking about incest, we ask, "What was it that
pulled us through?" I said it was my grandmother, my *obachan*,
who pulled me through. Then I realized that God was with my
grandmother—that she helped me to define somehow, in that
terribly lonely, despairing time, a spirituality that was beyond
the church, beyond Christianity—a connection with something

beyond that was there to help me survive. Maya Angelou has said, "You are here because somebody has loved you enough to make sure that you are here." That saved my life several times. When she reminded me that human beings are more alike than unalike, that saved my life. Whether we're blond and blue-eyed, yellow and narrow-eyed, black and brown-eyed, we're all part of a family, the human family. I didn't understand that until I reached fifty. And now as I become more experienced in this journey, I can feel that I'm able to make a difference, to help liberate other people—not just women but men and children, too—from this terrible cage called shame.

In 1984, my husband and I were invited to Hiroshima to take part in an international peace conference. Every year on August 6 in Hiroshima, there is a ritual to commemorate the people who were killed by the atomic bomb. They light a candle and float it in a lantern on the Motoyasu River, the river that flows through Hiroshima and is called "the River of the Dead." It was said that after the bomb was dropped, people who were dying of thirst and burns and radiation threw themselves into the river, which was full of bloated bodies for days thereafter. So every year, they float the lanterns—the light representing the souls who died, and also the light of hope that it will never happen again. I knelt to float the lantern and heard the soul of my grandmother's sister, who died in Hiroshima, calling me across the river, and I wept and I wept and I wept. I said to my grandmother, "Obachan, this is for your sister, but it's also for you." It was a moment of connection, I think, a connection through time (my grandmother had been dead for many years)—a sense of blessing in returning to her memory, to my ancestry, as painful as many of my childhood memories were. It was a moment of epiphany, reminding me that I was a part of something greater, a larger spirit, and that spirit was telling me to surrender to it, to give up control. And in that surrender is transformation, and in that transformation is grace.

COMFORT

❦ *Elizabeth Watson, 82* ❧

Elizabeth Watson is an ecofeminist theologian, an environmental activist, a lecturer, and the author of Guests of My Life, *which details her spiritual journey after the death of her daughter. She was born in Cleveland, Ohio, the granddaughter of a Methodist minister, and planned to enter the ministry herself, but she dropped out of graduate school at the University of Chicago Divinity School to pursue a nonprofessional ministry as a Quaker. For many years she worked in Chicago as a community organizer, working to improve relations among the races. She lives in Minneapolis, Minnesota, with her husband, George, a retired college professor. In addition to their three surviving children, they raised four foster children, and now have twelve grandchildren.*

Thirty years ago, my husband and I lost our oldest daughter in an automobile accident. She was, like me, a night person— I never could get her up in the morning, but she came alive in the evening. She had inherited from her father a sensitivity to light, so that from the time she was a girl, she had to wear tinted glasses to cut down the glare. A friend of ours, an Episcopal priest in Chicago, offered to say prayers for her in his church. In the English translation of the Latin requiem Mass, there is a recurrent phrase: "May light perpetual shine on her." When I heard this phrase, I thought, *Light perpetual*? Never to know the night sky, which meant so much to her? Never to delight in the movement of the stars and the planets, the phases of the moon, but to have *light perpetual* glaring down at her? That's the last thing my daughter would have wanted, the last thing I would ever want for her. I was trained as a Christian minister, but one of the knottiest arguments I had with Christianity was its tendency to see things in these dualistic, antithetical terms— light versus darkness, good versus evil. It was one of the things that ultimately caused me to abandon my plans to become a minister.

It seems to me intellectually naïve, as well as morally abhorrent, to see the world in terms of straight lines, rather than circles or spirals, to ignore the beautiful, rich complexity of the world and look at nature and human nature as something to be *controlled*. Christianity, Judaism, and Islam all teach that good and evil are locked in perpetual struggle, enemies of each other. They teach that good must overcome evil, that light must overcome darkness, rather than seeing that good and evil, light and darkness are parts of the whole. One cannot exist without the other.

My mother's father, whom I adored, was a Methodist minister of the old-fashioned Bible-pounding, hellfire-and-brimstone variety. The minister at my parents' church was dry and dull, but my grandfather was exciting, vivid, impassioned. I loved to go to his church. When I was seven years old, I asked him how he got to be a preacher. "God called me," he said. "Would God call me, too?" I asked, whereupon he told me the story of Samuel in the Bible, who as a child heard God calling him and prayed, "Speak, Lord, for thy servant heareth." So every night, I prayed, "Speak, Lord, for thy servant heareth." My grandfather taught me another way to be receptive to the idea of "God calling." "At the beginning of each day," he said, "close your eyes, open the Bible, and let your finger land on any random page; wherever it lands, that will be your text for the day." When I was eleven, my finger landed on the first verse of the fortieth chapter of Isaiah: "Comfort ye, comfort ye my people, saith your God." It was as if those words were engraved in fire into my brain. I was to comfort God's people, which I interpreted even then to mean *all* people, then later expanded to all living things, then later to include the earth itself. This was the beginning of my call to the ministry, which has shaped not only the inner events of my life but the outer ones, too. The concept that we have the opportunity and the responsibility to comfort people who are suffering has evolved over the years in many unexpected ways, but my journey has always been to try to be a channel to bring peace and comfort into the world.

I must have been an insufferable child—always reading and piously quoting the Bible for the edification of my not-very-interested schoolmates. Since most churches at that time did not give full ordination to women, everyone laughed when I said I was going to be a preacher. I would get taunted on the playground: "Girls can't be preachers." I turned inward, then, becoming more and more of a loner. Most parents worry because their children aren't good enough. My mother worried because I was *too* good. She felt that I was missing out on the fun of childhood. She also believed that it wasn't *seemly* for a young girl to aspire toward the ministry—she wanted me to be a bridge-playing, recipe-exchanging, gracious-living housewife. The minister of our church also tried to dampen my ambitions by steering me into religious education. But my father said over and over again, "Don't let anyone set limits on your ambition."

During the next few years, some terrible things happened. My little sister died in the night of whooping cough. My cousin's house burned down. My best friend's father lost his job. Then I saw a picture in the paper of Chinese children starving—I can still see the horror of it in my mind's eye. All of these things upset me terribly. My grandfather had taught me the last verse of the Fourth Psalm: "Now I will lie down in peace and sleep, for thou, Lord, makest me to dwell in safety." Somehow, the idea that God could let us dwell in safety was a mockery. Here were all these children—my sister, my friend, my cousin, the children in China—and why wasn't God taking care of them? This was the beginning of my realization that God is *not* almighty, *not* omnipotent, but limited, as we are, by the laws of cause and effect. After that, I never quite believed in the idea of safety ever again.

When I was a freshman in high school, my church sent me to a missionary conference, where I heard a very charismatic woman give a speech about Gandhi's advocacy of nonviolent resistance against the British rule in India. This woman, the wife of the Methodist bishop in India, spoke about the inconsistency of trying to make Christians out of Hindus, when Hinduism had produced a more Christ-like person than any Christian she knew. I was fascinated by what she said and sought her out at the hotel where she was staying. She spoke with me for several hours, recommending things for me to read and promising to keep in touch with me, which she did, for years. That's how the work of this great Indian leader first entered my life. From that time on—I was fourteen then—I saw myself as Gandhi's follower, consciously making the major decision to dedicate my life to nonviolence. And that has stayed with me for the next sixty-eight years, right up to the present day.

Later that year, during a public-speaking course, I gave a speech on—who else?—Mahatma Gandhi. My speech teacher took me aside to ask me if I would be interested in speaking on this subject outside the school. I thought, since I was called to the ministry, I'd better start practicing now. So my teacher became my booking agent, and I went out all over Cleveland to high school assemblies, luncheon clubs, women's organizations, church groups—you name it, I was there. And his faith that I had something important to say helped to deepen my commitment to becoming a minister.

I never had a date in high school. My closest friends were faculty members, who seemed to take a great interest in my intellectual and spiritual journey. But in college, I discovered *fun* for the first time. I majored in Greek, learned to dance, dated many different people, and fell in love with my husband. I was asked to join the university's speaker's bureau and traveled all over southern Ohio, conveying Gandhi's message of peace and nonviolence. One of my close friends was a black woman named Evelyn. I had become aware that she could not live in a dorm, she and her boyfriend could not go to a dance, there was not a place in town that she and I could go to share a Coke together. Enter Walt Whitman into my life: "By God," said Whitman, "I will accept nothing that all cannot have their counterpart of on the same terms." Every time I thought of that line, I substituted the name Evelyn for "all": "By God, I will accept nothing that Evelyn cannot have her counterpart of on the same terms. . . ." All my life, wherever I went, I asked myself, "If Evelyn were here, could she eat at this restaurant with me? Could she buy a house in this neighborhood?" And if the answer was no, then neither would I. So race relations became for me a primary arena to answer my childhood call to comfort God's people, whether it meant preaching in a church on Sunday or working for better race relations in America.

My husband and I were married after spending one year apart, since we had received scholarships to different graduate schools. It was a year of great intellectual excitement for me. The first week I was there, I heard the great theologian Henry Nelson Wieman speak about "process theology," which sees God as an integrative process at work in the universe and in human history. That was a very hopeful idea for me, and somehow fit in with my wish to bring comfort to people. But it conflicted with the orthodox view, which says that there are *chosen people*, and that only the chosen are eligible for redemption. The orthodox view sees Christianity as *the* major event in human history, whereas, as Wieman suggested, it seemed clear that God has been at work throughout human history, not just since the birth of Christ. And if Christianity excludes huge numbers of people—most of the people of the world, in fact, and even a Hindu in India who was as Christ-like as Jesus—what kind of a religion was it? Was the only way to God the Christian way? Aren't we *all* part of the human family? I belong to the Christian tradition, but reject the exclusive claim that it is the only path to God.

Spirituality does not mean religion only. Spirituality contains the idea of the journey, an acceptance of other people's journeys. It *includes*, rather than *excludes*. I am troubled by the strength of the religious right, not just in Christianity but in Islam, Hinduism, and Judaism, and not just in this country but as a negative, regressive force all over the world. I'm perfectly willing for people to believe what they want, but fundamentalists do not seem willing to let the rest of us believe what *we* want. The whole thrust of fundamentalism is on personal salvation: Endure the trials of this earth, be saved, and then "great will be your reward in heaven." They don't see the earth as *home*, but as a temporary place of tears and torment, from which they long to escape to a better place. They have lost sight of what an incredible planet we live on, how it is there for us to sustain us and nurture us with beauty and meaningful relationships. It's in our language: You treat someone "like dirt." So I'm concerned that we see the entire world as a holy place, in theological terms as the incarnation of God. God's presence on earth is manifest in all aspects of this incredible planet, in which we are all interrelated. We do not exist alone, but in coexistence with the animals and birds and fish and the creeping, crawling things, the mountains, the rivers, everything. When we allow a species to go extinct, we have also extinguished part of ourselves.

William Sloane Coffin said that preaching, opening yourself to be a channel for God to speak through you, is the most exciting thing in the world. That's one of the reasons why I always loved it so much. I was very skilled at it, and took perhaps too much pride in my ability to program other people's worship. I loved to create the kind of service where the hymns and responsive readings and Scripture lead inevitably up to the sermon, then end with a beautifully crafted benediction—I loved the elegance of that, the aesthetic pleasure. But in my second year of divinity school, my husband, George, and I went to a Quaker meeting. When Friends meet for worship, their worship is based on silence. Chairs are arranged in a circle or square, so that there are no ministers, no leaders or guiders of the service. Worshipers speak out of an incredibly deep silence, out of the group, spontaneously. Sitting in that profound silence, in that circle of Friends, gave me a feeling of *rightness*—the sense that Gandhi would have approved. We were aware that the Quaker church was one of the historic peace churches. The church we had grown up in had taught us that war was wrong. Then, with the arrival of Hitler and Mussolini, it said, "This war is different." George and I were looking for a spiritual home with a group of people who not only believed that war was wrong, it was wrong even if there was a war on: As Gandhi taught, it is wrong to kill any thing, under any circumstances, *ever*. I began to feel that the Society of Friends was calling me to a nonprofessional ministry, which could become my whole life, rather than merely a career. So it was about that time that my calling to give comfort shifted from becoming a minister to trying to do something to improve race relations and civil rights. I never went on to become ordained; I dropped out of graduate school and went to work at a settlement house, then later for a neighborhood organization that was organizing the community block by block for integration.

The turning point in my life was the day we dropped the bomb on Hiroshima; that was the watershed of history, as far as I'm concerned. The bomb was dropped during the morning rush hour with *no warning*. The appalling loss of life, the hideous devastation, the radiation sickness that went on for years and years—well, that showed me that the evil was not just *over there*, in Nazi Germany and fascist Italy and imperialist Japan, but it was in us, too. We are all mixed bags. The central belief of Quakers comes from John's Gospel: "The light that lights everyone who comes into the world." Therefore, as a Society of Friends, we have no enemies, and it is up to us to appeal to the light of goodness in all people, to have some compassion for what may cause someone to run wild. We can't stand there and say, "We are holy, you are not. We are on the side of righteousness, and you stand for evil. Therefore you are to be condemned." We are *all* part of the human family, all capable of evil. The whole community suffers unless we work to eliminate the causes that give rise to people like that—not monsters, but people just like you and me.

George and I bought a house in Chicago, in a neighborhood that Evelyn, if she were with us, could have lived. He loved his job as professor at Roosevelt University, and I was deeply involved in my job, politics, the church, the community. We had four children, then added four foster daughters to our family. And then a series of disasters overtook us. The first was the death of our oldest daughter. All my life, I had had a sense of God's presence. After the accident, I felt that presence withdrawn from me. I was furious at a God who could allow our beautiful, talented daughter to have her life cut off at twenty-three. For years I experienced a kind of spiritual devastation, in which there was no God in my life and, as far as I was concerned, would never be again. I sat for hours and read the poetry of Emily Dickinson, who shook her little fist in God's face and told him off: "Twice have I stood a beggar/ Before the door of God! . . . Burglar! Banker—Father!/ I am poor once more!" I began studying the piano again and would play the music of Mozart—Mozart, who had such a horribly frustrating, miserable life, and dying so young, and yet this incredible music poured out of him, music that speaks of a world of beauty and order, proportion and grace—a world that was also, now, withheld from me. But for those few minutes, engrossed in that music and its universality, I could forget.

During the months and years following the accident, I began researching the subject of other people who had lost children. I had never forgotten that my calling in life was to bring comfort and peace into the world, even through the period when I was unable to comfort myself. So I put together a book about six writers, each of whom wrote about someone who died young, and who collectively, one by one, moved me through the process of grief. That book needed to be written to help me reach out to others who had lost someone, to help *me* forget my own grief in the process of comforting someone else. It helped me to understand that grief is the human lot, never to be escaped, ultimately, by anyone. David, in the Bible: "Oh Absalom, my son, my son, would God that I had died for thee." Macduff, in *Macbeth*: "All my pretty ones? . . . What, all my pretty chickens?"

Dickinson: "Oh God/ Why give if Thou must take away/ The loved?" Very, very gradually, I come out of my withdrawal and into the acknowledgment that we must all cope with loss, maybe not through death, but loss of job, loss of self-confidence, loss of health, betrayal by someone we trusted. . . . In time I began to let go of the concept that God is all-powerful, and to see God as part of the human process, unable to help, just as I, as a parent, was unable to protect my children from encounters with evil, even death—so God, too, was suffering from the inability to step in and save the human family. The sense of God suffering with me, and with the whole human race throughout history, made me feel I was no longer alone in a meaningless, randomly evil universe. And I slowly, gradually experienced a newly *earned* sense of belonging to the human community in a new and far deeper way.

About every six or seven years, something terrible happens to me. Each time, I am asked by the universe to change my life, always in the direction of more spiritual depth, more *inclusiveness*. The accident happened in 1964. Six years later, I came down with pneumonia and became a semi-invalid. I was allergic to antibiotics, so my lungs did not fully heal. The air pollution in Chicago was so bad that we were told we must move or I might never regain my health. So George and I said to each other, "Well, maybe there's some lost cause we can get involved with." We sold the house we loved and George took a jab at a tiny, floundering college on Long Island, where, in my late fifties, a job came seeking *me*.

I was hired to work at the birthplace of Walt Whitman in Huntington, New York. I was to be a "Whitman presence" in the house—to saturate myself in his life and work, catalogue new acquisitions, and meet and discuss Whitman with any visitors who might stop by. Whitman was an ecofeminist. He always wrote in inclusive language; when he said "man," he included women, all ethnic groups, and all of society's outcasts, the lost ones. There were days when I was alone in the house, and a young man would walk up the driveway with a look on his face of coming to a shrine. Whitman was openly gay a hundred years ago and suffered terribly because of it, his books banned by libraries and his family ashamed of him. And I knew that this young man felt that somehow Whitman legitimized him. So I would take out all our treasures, the personal objects, the first editions, the manuscripts written in Whitman's own hand, and would spend the afternoon talking about him, quoting him, just giving myself totally to this person, because I knew that Whitman could give him a sense of his own worth. I couldn't comfort these men directly, but I could be a channel for opening up my love for Whitman, in order to give them the solace I sensed they needed. Sometimes they recognized this and thanked me; more often they did not. But giving solace doesn't depend of how it is received. The only thing that matters is the giving of comfort.

I never thought of myself as a particularly brilliant person. For many years, I deferred to my husband's intellectual superiority, what I thought of as his more logical, orderly mind. I had circular reasoning and gut feelings and intuitions, but I didn't think logically, the way I thought men did. It's true that I was able to hold my own at the seminary, where there was a lot of intellectual competitiveness, but it seemed to me that I had to work harder at it than the men did, and I always wished I had been given a better brain. Well, one of the great gifts that feminism has given me is the knowledge that a woman's way of knowing is just as valid, perhaps *more* valid, than a man's, because we see things more in terms of circles, relationships, synthesis, complexity, whereas men tend to see things in straight lines, goals, decisions, conclusions. It used to be that whenever I was in a group situations and had an idea, I held my tongue, thinking, "Oh no, they'll never accept this, it's too far out." So I wouldn't speak. And then I felt like such a coward for *not* speaking, which was an absolutely intolerable feeling for me. I'm out there now, with confidence in what I have to say, taking stands on what matters to me. I no longer have to worry that if I stick my neck out, my children will lose face among their peers, my husband's job might be jeopardized, I might embarrass my family, someone will laugh at my ideas. I'm freer than ever to be myself and say what I authentically feel.

Women, speak out. Stand up for what you believe. Go back to that teenage person you were, who *wanted* something very badly, then go out and get it. This is a time in your life when there's nothing and no one standing in your way. I remember the summer that I was married, which was also the year that my brother went away to college, and my mother went around all summer weeping, "My life is over, my children are gone and nobody needs me anymore." Chronologically, her life was only *half* over. There had always been an unresolved conflict between us: my rebelliousness and her inability to say to me, "I'm proud of you." I had always dreamed of a reconciliation with her, but she received a terrible concussion in the same accident that killed my daughter, and she entered a nursing home, not knowing me when I came to visit, and eventually died there. She never got over her anguish at losing her children, losing her role, losing her identity as a mother. I just wish I could reach her now, to offer her some words of comfort. She used to love music—I would urge her to go back and study the piano again. She used to work as a hospital volunteer—I'd help her continue her volunteer work, so she could forget about her own problems by giving comfort to someone, anyone. The reconciliation I hoped for never happened, but now I travel across the country giving workshops on what I call "Being a Crone," trying to comfort other older women who feel their lives are over. Maybe part of why I do it is because I can't reach her.

In 1984, I was diagnosed with cancer and was told I might

have five good years. Well, I've had eleven years, and they've been years of huge growth. I've become more and more aware of what's happening to the earth as I myself was suffering with cancer. I've grown in compassion, in humility, the humility to see that I am a small but integral part of the whole, rather than having always to be in charge. I think I've become a more comforting person. My life has been an unfolding, a circle or a spiral of infinite possibilities. From Whitman, I learned the concept of death as eternal recycling. He understood scientifically that the elements that make up our bodies were in existence from the beginning of the world, from the big bang. If we don't put our bodies in stainless-steel coffins and concrete vaults, they go back to the earth and become part of the ongoing life of the planet. Seeing life and death as eternal recycling has taken the fear out of death for me. No life can be lost. We don't go to heaven somewhere with golden streets and eternal bliss, but live on in the hearts of those we touched. As Whitman said:

> I bequeath myself to the dirt, to grow with the grass I
>   love.
> If you want me again, look for me under your boot-
>   soles
> You will hardly know who I am or what I mean,
> But I shall be good health to you nevertheless,
> And filter and fiber your blood.
> Failing to fetch me at first, keep encouraged.
> Missing me one place, search another.
> I stop somewhere, waiting for you.

SUBVERSION

✧ Sister Monica Weis, 53 ✧

Sister Monica Weis entered the convent of the Sisters of St. Joseph in Rochester, New York, at the age of eighteen. Trained as a high school English teacher, she obtained her doctorate in English at the age of forty and is now a professor of English at Nazareth College in Rochester, where she teaches classical rhetoric, eighteenth- and nineteenth-century American literature and methods for teaching secondary English. A trained singer and church organist, she relaxes by birding and hiking in the mountains.

My biggest problem when I was a young person was that I never allowed myself to be a human being: I was too busy being a human *doing*. I thought the busier I was, the more fully I was living, the more completely I was embracing life. You've got to *make it* in life—everybody says so. I think it comes from this peculiarly American culture we live in, the idea that we are nothing except what we *do*—the unconscious fear that if I stopped, there might have been *nothing* inside. I had forgotten, or possibly hadn't yet learned, that no matter what we *do*, there's already a self there, which also needs to be attended to. But I paid almost no attention to that until many years later, until I was almost forty.

My dad was an advertising executive, my mother a home-maker who had always wanted to be a nurse but had to leave grade school to take care of her sick father, then my sick aunt—she was a great caretaker of people. My dad was a competitive, hard-driving workaholic and a highly creative thinker, which gave me a lot of pleasure in and respect for the creative mind at work. My two brothers were twelve years and six years older than I; one was an artist and an introvert, the other an athlete and extrovert. So where did I fit in? It took me years to figure that out. I carved out a small territory for myself in music, studying piano for thirteen years, voice and organ for four years. As a musician, I was trained to give *performances*. In my family, the performance ethic was very important: Activity, production, accomplishment were the measures of a good life. My last recital was in college, when the psychic cost of being a competitive performer—practice, memorizing, rigor, stress, ego, the lime-light—became too much for me. I decided as a freshman not to do this performance thing anymore. But that performance ethic somehow translated itself to the academic, scholarly realm, and then later to the workplace.

I was in a complete fog in high school. Though I was active in clubs, choirs, and honors programs, I had no idea where I was going or what I wanted to do with my life. All I knew was that I wanted to be *more*. I had a vague sense of dedication, quite early on, to principled living—the feeling that I wanted to be of service, that I didn't just want to build up a little kingdom of my own, of *stuff*, and selfishness—but no clue what that meant. I also had a normal amount of sexual curiosity, and was always falling in and out of love—once with a guy in the army, to whom I used to write ten-page letters. After his discharge, I visited him in Syracuse, where he was going to morticians' school; whenever he took my arm, I always felt he was sizing it up to see what kind of embalming candidate I would make. At a recent high school reunion, another man, who was on his third wife at the time, a clarinetist with Pete Fountain's group in New Orleans, said, "You know, I was madly in love with you, but you would never look at me." Just think, I could have been his fourth wife! My most serious boyfriend was four years older than I; he was my date for the prom. I saw him recently—short, balding, little tufts of gray hair—and I thought, I could have been married to this guy! Somehow, these attractions always turned out to be infatuations, whereas I was, half-consciously, aiming at finding a *magnificent obsession*, a way to transcend the ordinary. I didn't just want to drift into marriage and motherhood and suburbia and two cars in the garage: I wanted more than that, always *more*.

We stumble into things. It may look like coincidence to people who don't have a great belief in the spiritual life, but I believe there is a providence that leads us to where we're supposed to go. In my junior year, one of my teachers asked me if I had ever considered a religious vocation. I said "No, never!"

The truth was that I *had* thought about it but felt myself unworthy. She said, "You're intelligent, energetic, principled, dedicated to this notion of *always going for the more*, doing the extra thing. You could very well have a vocation. Why don't you pray about it?" Almost immediately, my defenses collapsed; it was my first dynamic moment of being vulnerable to God. In praying, I said, "Oh, me? You want me?" Then there was a moment of saying, "I surrender." So I entered the convent at the age of eighteen, right after high school. Knowing nothing, I thought I could find transcendence through God, whom I experienced as *out there*, other. I had a long way to go in my own spiritual development. I didn't yet know what kind of a commitment I was making, or any idea of what it meant to live a "vowed life."

The vow of celibacy is a gift, and is defined as the gift of love to *many* people, in contrast to a single love relationship. It cannot be lived unless the gift of celibacy is there—or rather, it *can* be, but only at the risk of turning into a juiceless old prune. A medieval Christian mystic, Hildegard of Bingen, wrote about the juiciness of God, the fecundity of God, as expressed in all the richness of Mother Nature, the diversity, the *redundancy*, the overflowing of God's love as expressed in the natural world. This is the God I'm committed to. So, if my God is a juicy God, I had better be a juicy *person*—by loving people. And that can be expressed in many ways.

In my mid-thirties, I experienced a strong romantic attraction to a male friend and professional colleague. After several years, this attraction turned into love, and then we had to decide whether to express it or not express it in a way that wouldn't compromise either the love we felt for each other or our spiritual lives. Ultimately, we both had to rethink it and ask, "Is this what we want, or is the life we've committed ourselves to what we really want?" We had to redefine the relationship to embrace all aspects of ourselves, including our sexuality, and then face up to what we'd learned. And what we learned was that love is never bad, but that it does not always have to be expressed physically. Of course it was painful, at the time, and physically frustrating, but it helped me toward wholeness—like taking a diamond and polishing each of the facets.

There's no such thing as denying or giving up one's sexuality. I am a sexual being, which means that I am sexually attracted to people and will be until I'm six feet under. You can't deny it or skirt it, but simply face it, accept it. Human beings are complex, not simple. I think we have to struggle in order to find out who we really are—to uncover, recognize, and embrace all dimensions of ourselves, not just sexuality but everything we might rather not confront, such as, in my case, my tendency toward controlling or manipulating people. Sometimes, we'd prefer to edit out some of the more unpleasant pieces of ourselves—those shadows—but that is a move away from wholeness. The Greek historian Hesiod wrote about turning points in human life—moments he called *"kairos,"* which means a moment of transformation, of metamorphosis, after which nothing is ever the same. In the major religions, *kairos* happens when the Messiah comes. We all have those touchstone moments, three or four times in life when insight is gained, when the truth becomes manifest. That relationship was such a moment for me—a turning point toward *wholeness* for me as a person.

Another touchstone moment was when I found, or stumbled into, my vocation as a teacher. In my twenties, I was still so foggy that I had no idea what I wanted to do. At that time in religious life, we didn't choose a career, we were told what to do and placed somewhere. In the 1960s, after college, I was sent to a small junior high school in Rochester. For some reason, the principal of that school felt I had some ability in English and moved me into an experimental program where we were trying out some highly creative techniques, like team teaching and flexible scheduling, which are being rediscovered now, in the 1990s. The transformative element of those eight years was the freedom to make mistakes. We were like young horses, and this principal gave us our heads. If she thought we were getting in trouble, she was there to counsel, but she encouraged us to be creative, take risks; if it hasn't been done before, she said, think it through, weigh it, think of the consequences, then *do it*. *Dare to fail* was the message. And because of that freedom, wonderful creative things *were* happening. I discovered I had a talent for teaching English, and a love for it, and since I still believed that the only way to embrace life was to be a *human doing*, I kept up an incredibly frenetic schedule. I was teaching English, teaching humanities, teaching music, collaborating with the drama coach to put on operettas, running play rehearsals, and going to meetings every night. Sometimes I didn't get home until one or two in the morning, then got up at six to pray with my religious community and teach the next day. This went on for years, way into my thirties.

By this time, at the urging of that junior high school principal, I had gone back to school for my master's and begun teaching on the college level. Then I was told that if I wanted to keep my job, I would need to go back to school for a Ph.D., which I did, at the age of thirty-six. And that experience was the third, and perhaps most important, *kairos* moment for me—one of the most horrible experiences of my life, but probably the most transforming.

As an older woman, pushing forty, and the only woman religious (which is different from a religious woman) in a town of eighty thousand people, I felt marginalized during those entire terrible four years. I made friends outside the English department, but the doctoral program was composed almost entirely of hard-nosed, competitive young men, and the graduate English department was highly politicized. I had no experience of politics, and a kind of naïve misunderstanding of how systems worked. After living within a religious community for almost twenty years, I was confronting an ethic—competition—and a culture—political infighting—that was as alien to me as I must have been to them. So I was in a confrontative stance with the English department, and feeling absolutely bruised and embattled, and trying to find a way to get through it without getting psychically maimed.

After about a year and a half, I had a chance to review my records and discovered why they were giving me such a hard time. I was appalled to find two comments from former professors that just burned themselves into my soul. The first one said, "It will be interesting to see if we can do anything with her writing, but at the age of thirty-five, perhaps it's too late." The other comment was, "Not a great track record—not one to bet on for the next race." I saw these comments only once, but as you can see, I've memorized them. Now a new emotion entered my repertoire: anger. Anger at these guys—I always referred to them as "bastards" in my mind—who had turned me into a nag, a failed horse that couldn't even make it into the Kentucky Derby. I thought, "Okay, you bastards, I can outwait you. You can shovel out the grief, but my staying power, my perseverance, is going to be better than yours. I'm going to wear you down." Because I needed that doctorate in order to keep my job, and because I needed to prove to myself that my life was not over.

The way I got through it was by hard work and prayer. There was a parish nearby where I went every day at five o'clock for Mass, though I was at a stuck point or stalling point in my prayer life. Almost every day, I sat there crying, wondering how I could survive this. One day, I looked up and saw a plaque that depicted the Rock of the Resurrection, where the women went to Christ's tomb on Easter Sunday morning to embalm the body of Jesus, with the words "Who will roll away the stone for us?" And that became my prayer for those four years:

"Who will roll away this stone for me?" Another phrase was a quotation from Saint Paul: "Meanwhile, let us go forward on the road that has brought us to where we are." Meaning, I am here, and I can quit and go home and be accepted back anytime I choose. But I am *here*, in this terrible place, and there is some reason I'm here, some lesson I need to learn. Robert Frost said, "The only way out is through." You cannot skirt these things, you cannot, if you're going to be worth your salt, refuse the lesson. What lesson? Compassion, not competition. Reinforced by: I will *never* treat a student as I am being treated.

I decided to play their political game, but only on my own terms. While refusing to fawn over them, I stopped confronting the system directly. Instead, I sidestepped it—offering to rewrite B+ papers, volunteering to do oral reports, going over early drafts of my papers with my teachers before I handed them in. I didn't compromise my personal integrity, but did whatever was necessary to get all A's. So while that experience just stripped me down to the essentials, it never broke me, because in the process I had to face myself. Who was I? I was a woman close to forty, whose life, however, was *not* over. I was surrounded by a particularly toxic form of ageism and sexism, but that didn't mean I had to buy it. If the men around me thought that the pursuit of *knowledge* took precedence over everything, I knew that there must be *heart*, compassion in what I was doing. I felt very bonded to my congregation of the Sisters of St. Joseph, and that probably gave me the extra strength I needed to reach deep down and find the grit, the determination to keep on going and not quit. And when the four years were finally over and my work was done, I went home to heal.

It took me five years to feel completely myself again. The scars I still carry are learning scars: a reminder never to forget the lesson that was contained in the process of acquiring them. I hope I've been true to that. In the positions of power I hold, on boards, advisory boards, planning committees, I try to make sure that we as a group do not fall into that devastating pattern of competitiveness, but that our decisions are based on compassion and cooperation. The dignity of each person needs to be preserved. We try to get away from that destructive, dualistic thinking, in which there is one, and there is *the other*. There is *them*, and there is *us*. There is the winner's circle, and then there are all the losers—outside. And I think that's hooked up with the wisdom of growing older, when you begin to see that there isn't *the other*, but only *the one*. You are standing *with* someone, not in opposition to or as an adversary *against* him. There is no other. There is only all of us.

Thomas Merton said that it is necessary to see life in all its potential, "to obey life." To me, that means reverence for the amazing diversity of life, the recognition that all things are holy. We are all made of stardust. Stars that exploded billions and billions of years ago have showered down their cosmic dust here on earth. Therefore all of the energy of the cosmos is one. If I see the planet as a living, breathing organism, and myself as just one of the species on it, then I can feel how I am linked to everything out there, how when there is suffering, I suffer. All the problems of the world are *mine*.

The words *reconciliation* and *bridge building* are used to describe the mission of the Sisters of St. Joseph, which goes all the way back to 1650, but I think they are even more relevant today. When we try to reconcile opposing viewpoints, then build bridges of communication, we speak, not out of ego and arrogance, but out of an awareness that we are all connected to one another. I think this is particularly relevant now, in this multicultural, fragmented, highly politicized society—the kind of society that separates, rather than reconciles, that burns bridges rather than builds them. Until now, we've been under the delusion that everything in nature is to be exploited for the comfort or convenience of humans. But that's all changing now. Society as a whole is moving toward another moment of *kairos*, of transformation. And I believe that the metamorphosis is a good one, and long overdue.

Power does not welcome a challenge. There have always been and will always be entrenched systems, institutions, and structures that resist change, that punish dissent and innovation. Whenever there's a challenge to the patriarchal status quo, the old dogs in positions of power start howling, trying vainly to hold on to their comfortable livings. Their response is to dig in their heels, resist and obstruct the notion of change any way they know, until change *does* occur and everybody adjusts to it. Resistance to feminism, or any movement that empowers people, expresses itself in sexual harassment and all kinds of disrespect and abuse toward women. There are two ways of dealing with resistance of this kind: You can take on the structure, and probably lose, or you can be subversive and skirt around it. That's what women religious have been doing for hundreds of years.

There's a kind of anger that many people feel toward the Catholic church, which I think is unfortunate. All institutions tend to be stifling. Religion is not immune from forces that try to exclude, rather than include—forces that are driven, not just by the church, but by the whole secular patriarchal culture that we're caught in. The official power structure of the church has traditionally viewed nuns as the *cheap help* of the church, while only the males are in positions of power. The only thing that hits the press is the Pope saying that the issue of women priests is closed. No, it is *not* closed. You cannot stop people from discussing it, so you just laugh and ignore it and go on. There have always been ways of getting around the system, of saying, "Yeah, okay, you've got your power structure, you say we can't do this stuff, we'll find another way to get the job done. Something needs doing? Okay, we'll go do it. It hasn't been done before? So what, let's try." Unfortunately, when people leave the church, their information stops. They are no longer privy to these pockets of hope. So they can hold on to their anger for a long time, and see the church as never growing beyond the silly place it was when they got fed up. They lose hope, because they're out of touch. It's easy to criticize; more difficult to *construct*. But nothing will ever change if we all just pick up our toys and go home.

Theology is always growing and developing. Within religious tradition, there's a new model emerging, what theologians are calling "creation spirituality," or "green theology." There are Jewish, Protestant, and Catholic theologians now who are going back to the ancient texts and making a good case for the new thinking that we are all interrelated, interdependent. They're saying that it's been a misinterpretation of the Book of Genesis that we were meant to *subdue the earth*. Creation spirituality has a very long lineage, back to the Celtic Christians of the fourth century, when influential women of the church like St. Brigid were talking about our unity with the spirits in the forest; to the early fifth-century Benedictine tradition of the land ethic, which honored the rhythms of the land and the care for the seed, for farming; to the thirteenth century, when Francis of Assisi wrote so powerfully about his sense of unity with the birds and the animals, all the creatures of God's creation. . . . These traditions have always been part of the Catholic church, but haven't, until recently, been politically correct. They got lost in the whole sweep of patriarchal Western culture. Creation spirituality is scooping these traditions up again and saying, no, the earth is not there to be subdued, it's not there for *our* comfort and convenience; it belongs to everyone, the birds and the fish and the animals as well as *all* people. If I think of the planet as one breathing being, I understand that my eye is not more important than my foot, but each has a different role to play. Tensions between Jews and Christians seem to melt away when we say, "We are all part of the planet, so let's figure out how we as humans are supposed to fulfill our responsibility to it.

Let's not fight anymore over turf, but work together on something that affects us all."

There's a statement in one of the documents of the Sisters of St. Joseph that defines us as "Women who dare to undertake all," which I take to mean, "Women, dare to go where no one has been before." If feminism means being as human as you can, developing all your talents and making sure society makes room for their expression, then there has always been room within the Catholic church for feminism. It's always been in the tradition of the church to bring sisters out into the community, where they've become vital activists in the social arena, working to identify the needs of people, then finding a way to meet them. Within the Sisters of St. Joseph, we currently have a practicing lawyer, a practicing surgeon, chaplains at federal and state prisons . . . women who saw what needed to be done, then did it. Several sisters in our Rochester congregation have been arrested for civil disobedience over nuclear issues; they've got a rap sheet! Others have gone to corporate shareholders meetings and raised issues of social justice as a way to change the system. There are small hospice houses set up in the city that take only two people, because the state says if you have more than two, you have to follow all these state regulations, which would mean that a lot of dying people could not be helped. So the sisters said, "Okay, we'll take only two people dying of AIDS or cancer or whatever, but we'll house them in a bunch of places spread all over the city and do whatever we must to care for these people." Without drawing too much attention to yourself, you can circumvent the whole thing and get a whole lot done.

Nuns have always been countercultural. I'm not saying that culture is bad—I want to get out of that old Augustinian, Cartesian dualism—only that the culture tends to suck us into materialism, consumerism, and we're always trying to find the *more*: the spiritual dimension. We're always suggesting that science is not enough, technology is not enough, knowledge is not enough. Just because we *can* do it doesn't always mean we *should*. The special gift that women have is to offer an alternative to prevailing modes of thought, to insist that we examine the human dimension of things, the ethical dimension, the planetary dimension. And when the entrenched powers start howling, just quietly walk around them, quietly subvert, then work, in secret if necessary, but together, on a grass-roots level, to hold out another model. This, I think, is the pathway to change, not only in our own society, but throughout the world.

When I was very young, I used to think that old people somehow withdrew from life, my only view of age, from that long-ago perspective, being senility. We always used to joke about "grinning witlessly at each other over the half doors of the infirmary." That was always the phrase: "grinning witlessly." Now I see old age as a flowering, an opening and a deepening to the holiness of life. In youth, we try to make the world our oyster, to shape it according to our own ideals, needs, wishes, ambitions. As I've gotten older, I've grown far away from an interest in shaping the world; I'm much more interested in interacting with its rhythms, knowing that they are part of *my* rhythms. Buddha said that you don't have to be anything, you just have to be *aware*, be *awake*. I no longer feel that I have to be a *human doing*, but that being a human being is enough, more than enough. I'm more reflective, more willing to give up some control, which I now see as a defense mechanism, a way to avoid the messiness of life. I'm drinking deeply of every moment. I still use my music, still play for weddings, liturgies, celebrat- ations, but I no longer see it as performing or doing, but contrib- uting to the whole communal celebration. The performance ethic, I'm happy to report, is gone.

Many women go through a crisis of confidence at turning forty, fifty, but I say, Oh, no, no, no, no! Just embrace it, it gets better and better! In the forties, it's better, and in the fifties, even better! I think it's time to officially reject all those received ideas of what culture says to us: that we are old, unattractive, unimportant, invisible. Maybe it's time to bond together to create our own culture. Turn the television off. Throw out all our magazines. Put together a bibliography of books that validate the growing-old experience. Take a small patch of garden and cultivate it. Think small. Remember the lesson of the pebble: If you drop a boulder into a stream, it plops and sinks, swamping everything in its wake. If you skim a pebble over the stream, it causes a gentle ripple effect. We're all so interconnected that every little thing we do can have an impact. New models are possible, and they are happening. Maybe, if we all did this, not in a fighting spirit, but in a spirit of reconciliation, the walls would come tumbling down.

SOMETHING TO
HANG ON TO

ϲᴥᴏ *Marva Collins, 59* ᴏᴥᴖ

Marva Collins, a renowned educator in Chicago, Illinois, is the founder of the Westside Preparatory Schools, in which inner-city students are given a classical education, beginning at the age of four. A member of former President Bush's National Council on Education, she refused two presidential offers to become Secretary of Education. A sought-after speaker and lecturer, she has appeared on 60 Minutes *four times, is the recipient of thirty-nine honorary doctoral degrees, and has been the subject of articles in hundreds of periodicals, including* The New York Times, The Wall Street Journal, *and* Time *magazine. She has three children and two grandchildren.*

If I ever leave this house, I will give away all my Oriental furniture, all my antiques, all my possessions and walk out with a few pieces of clothing. There's so much responsibility involved in owning things: They need cleaning, they need polishing, they tend to accumulate and cause clutter, they weigh you down. Of far greater priority to me now is what I can give away. Yesterday, on my way to work, I saw a terribly ragged old man curled up on the street in front of Walgreen's. He was wrapped in a ratty blanket and silently rocking back and forth. I gave him what I happened to have with me at the time: a warm blanket—I keep a blanket in the car because of the horrible winter we had last year—a box of graham crackers that I was taking to the kids at school, and fifteen dollars in my purse. It was such a relief for me to give away what I had, not to be thanked or appreciated, just to give away what I don't really need anyway. Every *thing* can be replaced. That old man cannot.

In the last three years, I've begun to form an entirely new definition of success. As we begin dealing more and more with mortality, we begin thinking more of eternity, not the things that exist in time, the trappings of success. I've been to huge empty palaces, with no warmth or children in them. The glittering designer ball gowns, the houses, the cars mean much less to me than they used to. I realize I could live happily in one room, provided I could have my family around and frequent visits with my two grandchildren. Of course it's nice to be invited to the White House, to Camp David, very nice to get a standing ovation, but lately, thinking back, I noticed something missing in these occasions. I wonder if our hearts are really there, or if we're doing certain things for show, for political correctness. People seem to be saying what they think they should say, doing what they think they should do, but when a person really has his *heart* in his words, you can see the truth shining out. If the heart isn't there, you can see that, too.

I love being the age I am, fifty-nine. I wish I could freeze this age. My parents brought me up to be terribly responsible, to take care of things that were on my plate, to concern myself with other people and try to make a nice appearance. I'm still responsible, and still care about what people will think, to the extent that I don't want to hurt anyone's feelings, but I have a sense now that I know who I am, know my style, and don't wait for acceptance by others. I've stopped going to the beauty parlor, just shampoo my hair and pull it back. Who's got time anymore to get a manicure? It took a long time to get to this point, and I treasure it, treasure the confidence and the experience I have finally acquired after all these years.

I never really understood the empty nest syndrome. I don't regret a thing about those years of taking my daughter to ballet and my son to dramatic lessons and going to PTA meetings, helping them with their homework, talking to them, reading to them, shopping with them, getting their meals, doing their laundry, but it seems so obvious that every mother should be delighted when her children leave the nest and start their own lives. I love all my children and take great pride in their achievements, but I wouldn't want to retrace those years of youth, mine or theirs.

The hardest things that have happened to me taught me the most, both about myself and my enemies. An article appeared in the *Chicago Tribune* that contained all sorts of untruths about me and the school—that we cheated on our test scores, that we did something illegal in order to get federal funds—and it was deeply painful for me, personally, and caused the school a great deal of damage. The day the article appeared, I sat down and prayed that if I was doing something wrong, I wanted to let the school end. Afterward, I felt a great sense of peace wash over me. The animosity I had felt toward this reporter disappeared, even though my whole life, my integrity, my reputation, and all the work I had ever done were being attacked. A few months later, this same reporter who had been so unjust to me lost a child to AIDS. When I called him to offer my condolences, he burst into tears, saying that of all the people who had called, this call meant the most to him. My children asked how I could be kind to this man who had been so cruel to me. I told them that I can't let hate control my actions. Hate and rage destroy the person who feels these emotions, much more than the one who's causing them. I believe that my enemies do me honor, because they're the ones who make me strong, not the ones who treat me well.

Often, when traveling, I find that I am the only black person in the hotel who is not an employee of the hotel. Sometimes, other guests will approach me and ask me to iron their dress or do their laundry, shine their shoes, something like that. I just pat them on the shoulder and say, "I'll be right back." Or when I'm shopping in a department store, another customer will assume I'm a clerk and ask me the price of something, and I just say, "It's all free today, take whatever you like." At one time I would have become enraged at this presumption, but since I've gotten older, I've learned to pick my battles to avoid battle fatigue. My time and strength are limited, too limited to feel rage at every careless person who insults me. I need to conserve my strength to do what I'm supposed to do.

It's so easy to miss the point of why we're put on this planet. There's a famous story about Emerson and Thoreau, where Thoreau was on his deathbed and Emerson asked him, "Have you made peace with God?" Thoreau replied, "I don't remember arguing with him." That's me. I have no argument with God. I think the conditions we have to struggle with are there for a reason, even when we don't know what the reason is. So we're not told why we're here, but we better do the best we can, while we *are* here, to find out.

I think what Thoreau meant when he said, "I went to the woods to live more deliberately" was that people need solitude in order to concentrate on developing their inner resources. I don't want to wait until my last day on earth to ask myself the question, "Why was I put on this earth?" I want to find out way before that. That's why it's so important to meditate, pray, have solitude and time to think. At our school, we teach *The Odyssey* to eighth graders. We ask them: "Why did all the ships except Ulysses's crash into the rocks when the sirens were calling?" The answer:" Because he taught them how to plug their ears." There will always be the siren call of the drug dealers and the gangsters. You have to have enough inner strength and determination inside you to know when to plug your ears, to resist the beautiful, dangerous song of the sirens.

This is a country that treasures *things*. A lot of lonely people gravitate toward the superficial—money, fame, glamour. Things can't take the place of doing the inner work. Public victory can't replace private serenity. We need to be quiet so we can live more deliberately. Shut out the noise and distractions of the outside world so we can think about what matters and *focus* on how to make it happen.

I'm always quoting my favorite line from *Moby-Dick*: "In this slippery world, we all need something to hang on to." Once, I took my grandson to the playground. While he was swinging on the swing, I said, "Hold on, Sean, in this slippery world we all need something to hang on to." One day, he was climbing up the steps from my basement and he said, "Grandma, you should put railings here, because in this slippery world we all need something to hang on to." A lot of people don't have anything to hang on to when the bad times come. When I train teachers how to teach the story "The Three Little Pigs," I tell them straw houses and stick houses are fine if the weather is good, but when bad times come, we all need something to hold on to. The extra effort it takes to build the brick house pays off, because no matter how beautiful the weather looks right now, you can be sure that a storm will come.

We try to teach the kids about the basic law of economics: You become overdrawn at the bank if you don't have enough deposits. You have to constantly read—that's a deposit—you have to listen to other people, you have to look closely at nature and learn from the plants. In my garden, the clematis are dormant now, and they look so ugly with all those thick brown vines sticking out. But I know they will regenerate, just as human beings have the capacity to regenerate. By June, they'll be blooming all over the fence. People, too, can remain dormant for a large part of their lives, depending on their belief systems, or their beliefs will determine whether they will grow and thrive. Looking at the Grand Canyon or the stars, we make a deposit. We learn that we're not as important as we think. Every mountain, every rock has a history of thousands of years. The seasons change, teaching us that our time on earth is finite, so we'd better get started on living deliberately. If you keep on making deposits of this kind, you invest in yourself, and that's the most important kind of investment you'll ever make.

I don't think you can convey wisdom to other people. They have to earn it for themselves. Nobody can give me a map. I have to make my own. As teachers, we try to warn younger people about the pitfalls they will meet, and then we watch their eyes glaze over with boredom; they're absolutely not ready to hear it. Then five years later, they'll step in a hole and say, "Oh, this is the hole she was talking about." That's what we call education: teaching them to be mapmakers.

I've always had an idea about creating the perfect school. I'd take about a hundred kids between the ages of four and twelve away from the city for a few years, to a large piece of land out in the country, where we'd have a big garden, no television, no radio, and no newspapers. We'd all have dinner together—dinner has been taken from kids, either because the parents are very successful and busy or too poor and demoralized to bother—and talk at the dinner table about what we read that day. Every night, several of the children would prepare an intellectual talk for the group. It would be their job each day to discover something for themselves and thereby discover the miracle that is within each of them. They could study the rose to learn how unique each and every rose is. Until kids decide, "I am a miracle. I am unique. There is no one else exactly like me," they can never draw the conclusion, "Because I'm a miracle, I will never harm another person who's a miracle like me." In this slippery world, they all need something to hang on to.

In our family, we all have prominent noses. My kids always swore that when they grew up, they were going to have their noses fixed. And I said, "Go right ahead, pick some nose from a catalog, but just remember, that nose of yours is your heritage, it's your family trait, it's part of what makes you unique." So far, none of the kids have had their noses fixed.

ONLY YOUR REGRETS

❧ *Anna Kainen, 82* ❧

When Anna Kainen was growing up in Romania, she was forced to leave grade school at the age of seven. As a teenager, after immigrating to the United States, she went to work in a dress factory in Brooklyn to support her family. In 1975, at the age of sixty-two, after forty-seven years of unremitting factory work, she fulfilled a lifelong dream by entering City College as a freshman, graduating five years later. Since then, with the help of a grant from the Barbara Deming Memorial Fund and two writing fellowships from Columbia University, she's written two novels, twenty-five short stories, two hundred poems, five plays, and six essays, many of them published. She has divorced twice and has a daughter and two grandchildren.

... I hear the bells of childhood dreams. I walk by the waters. I sit alone at midnight listening to the waves ... I have been away. I am returning. Deep inside of me, there is this longing. What do I long for? Whose fingers do I want to touch my face? Whose face do I want to cup in my palms? What psalms and hymns do I want to sing? ... Shadows move, changing the face of the night, but there is no fear in me. ...

—Anna Kainen

My life didn't start until I was sixty-two years old. Until then, I was an unhappy, bitter person. I felt as old as the hills, like I had the weight of the whole world on my shoulders. My life since then has been a process of getting younger, of every year throwing off the unnecessary baggage of the past, until I was finally able, in my sixties, to come into my youth.

In my sixties, I found my first taste of freedom. My earlier life was spent living according to other people's expectations of me: my parents, my husband, my family. When your family doesn't need you anymore, that's frightening, but freeing. There's freedom in living alone and finding out who you really are. There's time to explore and contemplate what you've learned so far. And there's a duty to send out some of those messages so that other people can benefit from all the difficult lessons you've learned. For those of us who have lived a long time hold a key to all the generations that follow.

My origins are Romanian, Jewish, and poor. In Romania,

it cost tuition to send a child to school, so my mother took me out of school when I was seven. She told me I didn't need it for my future. My two brothers had to make a living, but I just had to get married. I pleaded with her to let me stay in school. She said, "Wait till we get to America, you'll go then." I waited eight years, until my father got enough money to send for us.

The worst thing that ever happened to me was my father leaving us to go to America. In my family, he was really the only one who loved me. He used to write letters to us, but after a few years, the letters stopped. Later I found out that he had become ill, had lost his job, and was ashamed because he didn't have any money to send us. In Romania, we lived on charity from my mother's parents. Those were terrible times for me. I was home all alone, my brothers were in school, and I used to run to meet the mailman every day. Even the mailman felt sorry for me when, day after day, there was no letter from my father. I felt that my father had lied to me and abandoned me. And then, eight years later when I came to America, I found a broken old man. I withdrew from him. I think I was trying to punish him for abandoning me, and that is a terrible regret for me, one I have to live with to this day.

We came to America, the promised land, when I was fifteen. We lived in one room above a bakery infested with rats. There wasn't enough money for a bed for me. My parents shared one bed, my two brothers another, and I slept on six chairs moved together. My father was old and worn out. My older brother got rheumatic fever. I was the only one who could work. So it turned out that I wasn't able to go to school then.

I got hired at a dress factory in Brooklyn for twelve dollars a week, twelve hours a day. I tried to go to night school after my working day, but eventually the strain caught up with me. I was so disappointed, I stopped talking. When I wasn't lying down or crying, I roamed the library, reading everything I could get my hands on, desperate to learn. The doctor called it a nervous breakdown, and it was true, it was a sickness of the soul, not the body. I was so unhappy, I thought I would never recover. But my whole family was depending on me for the money to eat, so I went back to work at the factory.

I was always trying to climb up and climb out. I finally got married at the age of twenty-eight to a man who thought he was an intellectual. I thought so, too. Here I was, nothing but a shop girl myself, but I refused to go out with anyone who just worked in a factory. I thought it was beneath me! So I married this man who was trying to be a writer but couldn't help support the family. After my daughter was born, I stayed working in the factory. By this time, I got a raise, I was making thirty-five dollars a week.

My husband had formed a little group of men who were trying to be writers, too. I used to eavesdrop on their meetings, listening in, very interested, and started writing myself. Once, I showed him a little poem I wrote, and he hated it, told me it was the worst piece of writing he ever saw. That stopped me from writing anything again for about twenty-five years.

The marriage was miserable, but I didn't know how to leave. I would ride the subways all night, back and forth from Brooklyn to Manhattan. I thought my child needed a father, even one who was abusive to both of us. We finally got divorced after twenty years, and two years later I got married again, a marriage that was worse than the first. For some reason, my second husband didn't approve of my daughter. He didn't want "his" money (the money I was earning in the factory) to be spent on gifts for my two grandchildren. Once in a while, he would hit me. But this time, I got smart, I didn't wait so long, I divorced him after seven years.

After my second marriage ended, I knew I would never get married again. I realized that it was now or never, that it was time I came into my own. Always, I had done for others. Now it was my own life I had to pay attention to. So I said, "That's it, kid, the rest of your life is going to be for you."

I decided that I was finally going to get an education. After getting my high school equivalency diploma, I took early retirement from the factory and entered City College in 1975, majoring in English. Oh, how I gobbled up all that literature! Shakespeare and Chaucer and John Donne, Hemingway and Thomas Wolfe and Jane Austen, the Brontës, Keats, Browning, I swallowed them all as if they were food, and I was in a kind of delirium, loving these books so much. And slowly, tentatively, I started writing myself. I remember when my first short story was accepted for publication, I went to the mailbox and saw the SASE I had sent, expecting another rejection. But the story had been accepted. First I went upstairs to my bedroom and cried. Then I called my daughter. Then I sat right back down at the typewriter.

Around this time, I got enough confidence to answer an ad in the *Village Voice*. "Mature, intelligent man seeks mature woman for companionship and friendship." People say you can't fall in love when you're old, but it's not true. I met Ben when I was already well into my sixties. And even though I'd already divorced two husbands, I realized that I had never really been in love before.

We met at a restaurant in the Village. We drank a little white wine and ate a lot of lobsters, then talked for hours. He was so good-looking, with a little Vandyke beard and beautiful bright eyes. We seemed to hit it off right away. And immediately I was so thrilled, because I had finally found someone I could feel comfortable with, even in silence.

Before I answered the ad, I was a little frightened. What is an old lady doing answering an ad? I said to myself. But then I thought, Go ahead, be brave, what have you got to lose? And then when I met him, I forgot I had even been afraid before.

We went on vacations every summer to a little house in Wainscott, near East Hampton, New York. After forty-five years of labor, it was delicious to sit in a hammock in the backyard, to plant a few flowers and to stare at the ocean. I had never had any leisure time in my entire life, never even known what leisure was. But those summers in the cottage, I had time to treasure the acute sweetness of that time with Ben. No, it's not true that you lose your capacity to love in later life. On the contrary, it's the very shortness of time, the nearness to death, that increases the intensity of your happiness. When you're young, there's always too much time, infinite time, so much that you can throw it away, waste it, kill it. When you're old, you feel that adolescent intensity again, but for a different reason. You know time is running out, and therefore you live every moment of happiness with a sense of profound gratitude.

We had five years together. He was eight years older, and I knew that he had serious diabetes and couldn't have too much time left. But those five years were long, and their effects lasting. When he died, I understood that at least I could say I had one love once. And I feel he is waiting out there somewhere for me, blessing me, as I am blessing him.

In the first five decades of my life, I died a thousand times, but somehow, in my sixties, I found new life, and strengths I didn't know I had. I always seem to manage, like a jack-in-the-box, to jump back. I caught pneumonia five times in the last three years. I've got glaucoma, cataracts, shingles in the eyes. Three cataract operations and maybe another one needed. On those terrible days when I feel I might go blind, I wonder if I could really live without reading, without writing. Then I think, My eyes are going, but as long as I still have a mind to think, there's always more to accomplish. My next project is to gather all my short stories into a collection.

I always tell people who are depressed about getting old,
Do what you really want to do and don't let anybody stop you,
and that will make you feel as though the world is really yours.
Do your dream, go for it, do it now! Take a chance, speak up,
what can you lose? Only your regrets.

MAGIC

✍ Laurie Cabot, 63 ✎

Laurie Cabot, a Druid high priestess, has been a practicing witch for over forty years. Born in Oklahoma and raised in Anaheim, California, she moved to New England when she was thirteen. As the founder of the Witches' League for Public Awareness and the author of three books on witchcraft, she travels widely and gives lectures and seminars on the science of witchcraft. Laurie is known as the "Official Witch of Salem." She lives in Salem, Massachusetts, with her two daughters, Jody and Penny, both also witches.

My interest in witchcraft began early, in my early teens. As a child, I had already experienced many psychic incidents without any idea of what they meant. I seemed to be able to see things so clearly, to hear in my mind things that other people were thinking. I could tell when someone was lying or when someone was in trouble. At about twelve, I began spending afternoons at the library, studying the science of psychic phenomena. The librarian there was a woman named Vivian, from Kent, England, who helped with my investigations into the psychic and spirit realm and guided me to the study of comparative religion and beyond. With Vivian's guidance, I began studying the theology and mythology of the Druids, which I learned later is the religion of *Wicca*, witchcraft. The Druids practiced witchcraft as a nature religion, much like Native American religion, with many gods and goddesses but no Satan or devil, since it predates Christianity by hundreds of years. The idea of *magic*, which is really nothing more than the transfer of psychic energy from one body to another, intrigued me greatly. Later I learned that Vivian was herself a witch.

At sixteen, I became initiated as a Celtic witch, which involved taking a vow with a high priestess. There were three people present at the initiation, representing the Triple Goddess in her three incarnations: the Maiden, the Mother, and the Crone. We cast the magic circle, and then, in the Kentish tradition, I was handed a sword, which is a magic wand like Excalibur, not a weapon. I held the sword upright against my breast, scooped some earth from inside the circle and placed it in a cauldron, representing the female principle, and took a vow to preserve the earth, to honor the ancient gods and goddesses, and to always give my wisdom back to Mother Earth. Then I turned the sword around and plunged it into the earth.

After my initiation as a witch, I forgot about it for many years. First of all, it was then illegal to practice witchcraft. Very few people, then and now, knew that a witch was not a Satanist. Also, at sixteen, love and sex, romantic ideas and adventures take precedence over matters of the spirit. Glamour, physical attractiveness, sex appeal, being "interesting"—all of that had a huge importance for me at that age. And because of that so-called glamour, it happened that I often attracted the wrong men. Not until much later did I find out how dangerous it is to rely too much on physical attractiveness, to look to men to provide the security that we can only provide for ourselves. In my generation, you weren't anything except what your husband was. Every woman's goal was to find a man who could take care of her. So I got married young and forgot about witchcraft for a long time.

My first marriage lasted a year and a half. He was an Italian, a fascinating, highly sexual man, as opposite from my stern Victorian father as possible. All my friends were getting married and having children. I thought I was madly in love. But there was no compatibility between us. He was a "man's man," totally focused on "the guys," on baseball and football games, a typical Italian male. There was no possibility of equality between us, and that was what I wanted most in a marriage.

My father was a wealthy entrepreneur, an elegant, old-fashioned drunk—I never saw him without a shirt and tie—and very traditional and chauvinistic. He was the masculine principle in the house. My mother and I were the mere females. My mother was subservient and subordinate to my father in every way except one: in her teaching of me. She tried to teach me to be me, to stand up tall and do anything I dared to do. But somehow, subtly but powerfully, I got the message that life was dangerous, that you couldn't trust or be sure what was going to happen next, that power resided somewhere *out there*, not inside. Especially if you were a woman.

After the divorce, I lived near my parents and stayed home with my daughter, did meditation to stay conscious and awake and balanced, and to decide what I wanted to do with my future. I painted a little, but nothing really called me. So, not knowing what else to do, I got married again, to a man who adored my daughter, wanted to be a politician, loved to laugh and dance and have fun, was again into "the boys," and was utterly feckless about money. My parents were comfortably upper-middle-class, and when they died, I inherited quite a bit of money, then immediately lost it all by giving it away to my second husband, who in turn lost it by a series of bad investments. It's the classic example of a woman giving away her power to a man. At the age of thirty, I divorced my second husband and then went through the darkest period of my entire life.

Money—the getting it, the keeping it, the taking care of it—has been a major theme for me, an area that I've resisted against all reason. It seems that I'm always either denying it, ignoring it, or worrying about it, until I suddenly find myself in desperate circumstances. That's what happened after my second marriage ended. Suddenly I was down to the very bottom of the barrel, with two children to support, no one to help, and *nothing*, absolutely zero. At the absolute nadir of desperation, I reached deep down and found my strength, asking all those questions that we all must, at some point, ask: "Who am I? What am I? Where am I going from here?" That's when my mother's teachings, and all my teachers' teachings, kicked in. I understood that I could not allow my children to starve, or myself to quit. So I was forced to go on welfare for two years.

There was no other alternative. I began to create, *by magic*, ways to survive and get along. One day, after paying the rent, I had exactly four dollars to last me for the week ahead. There were no groceries in the house except some macaroni, some tomatoes, and some peanut butter. So I made a spell to the Mother Goddess to please help me feed my children. I stood in line at a butcher shop, and when it came my turn, approached the butcher and whispered to him, "This four dollars has to last a week. Will two dollars buy a small piece of pork and a piece of beef to make spaghetti sauce?" He nodded, stepped back behind the counter, and started cutting meat. And cutting and cutting and cutting and cutting. I thought it was for some other customer. He handed me a piece of paper and said, "Pay over there." The cashier said, "That'll be four dollars." The blood drained out of my face. I had hoped at least to hang on to two dollars. To my shock, the butcher presented me with two enormous shopping bags entirely filled with meat. Then he put something in my hand, saying, "Give this back to me when you have it." He had given me a ten-dollar bill and enough meat to last two months. The next Monday, when the welfare check came, I ran down and gave the ten dollars back. It was like a gift from the gods. I wondered if that meant my magic spells were working.

I used those two years on welfare as a time to find a way to make money doing what I wanted to do. Another marriage was out of the question. My daughters needed the heritage of a strong woman so that they could stand on their own two feet, to marry if they chose to, but not because they *needed* to. Again I sat down and asked myself, "Who am I, what am I, and what am I going to do with the rest of my life?" First was the answer: I am a witch, that is my inner soul and my being, my spirit is a witch. I understood my myth, had been developing my psychic senses and using my healing abilities, and always followed the threefold law: Everything you do, whether bad or good, comes back to you threefold. I had done a lot of charitable work, donating money to ecology groups and antiwar groups and the churches of Selma, Alabama. So in a way, I was acknowledging the power I already had. I decided, no matter how short a life

I might have as a consequence, not to hide it any longer, to dress in the clothing of my priestesses and never take them off. That alone eliminated many options, in terms of making a living. I knew no corporation would ever hire me in my caftan and cape—a power suit, of sorts, but one that would not exactly fit into the corporate culture of IBM.

A friend suggested that we pool our resources and buy a house somewhere in the suburbs so our children wouldn't have to live in the city. I told her I would move anywhere in Massachusetts except Salem. Then she told me she had found a beautiful, sprawling eighteen-room house on Chestnut Street, one of the most architecturally perfect streets in America. That's how we happened to move to Salem. The house was right across the street from the then-mayor. And I wore, and kept on wearing, my long black dresses and my huge gold pentacle, but most people thought I was Jewish, because that pentacle looks like a Jewish star.

I've always had several cats. One of them, not too bright, kind of silly, got caught in a tree. No one would help me get her down—the fire department, the police department, and the Animal Rescue League all said she would come down by herself, that they had never seen a cat's skeleton in a tree. Every day, my other cat, Sabrina, would climb the tree, kiss her, turn around, and try to show her the way down. Finally, after three days and three nights, it began to storm. I called the *Salem Evening News*, and, in a very quiet, ominous tone, said, "My name is Laurie Cabot. My cat is in a tree. None of the city bureaucracies will help me get her down. It has been three days and three nights. I am a witch. That cat is my familiar. I want her down. *Now.*" That scared the hell out of them. Within fifteen minutes, the fire department had arrived, the police department, the Animal Rescue League, a representative from the mayor's office, along with the reporter and a photographer from the newspaper. The guy from the mayor's office said to the photographer, "What does *she* want here?" All I wanted was my cat back. The man from the Rescue League reached out the bathroom window with a long pole with a little loop at the end, looped the cat, and brought her in. It took exactly five minutes. Meanwhile, they were all saying, "Please don't zap us, please don't hex us." I stood at the bottom of the tree and gave them a lecture on what a witch is and what a witch isn't.

It's hard to explain to someone who has never ever seen a witch, who knows nothing but a Walt Disney witch, or the Christian horror of witches as the servants of Satan, that our religion forbids us to do any harm to any living thing, even to inanimate objects, because everything on earth is at least as important as humans are. I told them about the threefold law: If you harm someone in any way through magic, that harm will come back to you, multipled by three. It's a nature religion, worshiping the moon, the sun, and yourself, connecting yourself to the universe and everything in it. It's about respect and self-respect. It's always been our religion to respect the earth, to protect her, to preserve, to nurture, to replant, to clear the air, to not litter, to not pollute. . . . Anyway, I gave the entire assembled audience this fiery lecture on witchcraft, and the next night, pictures of our whole household appeared in the paper with the headline: SALEM'S BEAUTIFUL PEOPLE. That's how, whether I actually chose to or not, I "came out," finally and irrevocably, as a witch.

I was dealing with the question of how to make a living as a witch. Teaching classes was my first choice, but in the beginning there wasn't a great demand for Witchcraft 101. No one wanted a book written—"No one will read it," a bunch of editors told me. So I continued to create magic spells that would help our family survive—not focusing on money, because one of the rules of witchcraft is to project for stability and security but not for great wealth, fame, or fortune. Those are just offshoots of one's life goals, not the goals themselves. My goal was teaching and writing. I was able to get a few jobs teaching at local night schools, but it didn't pay enough to support us. So as a result, reluctantly, I started doing psychic readings and counseling, which I had no interest in or aspiration for. But it turned out that economic necessity forced me into learning what my true path was supposed to be.

One weekend, I canceled all my readings but one. One of my friends, a high priestess who was dying of cancer, was waiting for me to help her walk into the other world; I was going to hold her and talk to her and help her depart. I was glad to do it, sad to do it, totally emotionally tied up in helping her. But there was one reading that day which, for some reason, I didn't cancel. A woman in her thirties walked in and sat down in front of me with tears in her eyes. She said, "I don't want to talk about myself. I only want to hear about my son. He was eighteen and died suddenly two weeks ago in a car accident." I agreed to do whatever I could to help her, even though I wasn't sure I was qualified. All of a sudden, like Whoopi Goldberg in *Ghost*, I could see him standing next to her. "Your son is standing next to you," I said, describing him precisely: his red hair, his gray eyes, and so forth. I explained to her how Druids see the other world—that after we die, humans have the choice of remaining on earth as a ghost, being reincarnated, or going to the Druid heaven, the land of milk and honey, which we call Summerland. "Your son has decided to stay with you until it's your time, which will be a long time from now, because you are going to have a long life," I told her. Suddenly, her son thrust a sword at me, saying, "Tell my mother this is my most prized possession." When I told her, she gasped. She had buried him in his casket with his great-great-grandfather's sword. Just before she left, I told her, "Your son wants you to know that he's going to live forever, because he feels just like the High-lander." She said, "That's the last movie we watched together before he was killed." Of course I had no way of knowing that. She walked out smiling. And I felt that I finally had the proof of my religious beliefs.

Belief is a hard word for me. I have a science mind. I like proof, evidence, documentation. How could I have known about that sword? I must have half-expected her to say, "What sword, so what, it means nothing to me." After that reading was over, I ran to my friend and told her the story, saying, "Marie, we're really going to walk into the other world together. That woman came to me for a reason. We know, now, that it's real." So I passed the magic circle around her, and held her, and took her hand, and my spirit went with her into the spirit world, into Summerland. She did it with grace, with a smile on her face. And from that point on, I began to trust my own psychic abilities, which I had always used, but never entirely with full belief. That knowledge, that belief, never again left me.

From that time on, I knew I had found my power, my spirit, my strength. I could love freely, have a relationship freely, but knew my family could survive without *needing* someone else to take care of us. I was so connected to my spirit, it was like being a goddess. Around that time, I wrote a poem to my mother. "Mother, I thank you for your creative strength and sensitive nature, for inciting in me the power to stand like a goddess, against all odds. Mother, I see your beauteous spirit in all seasons. The white silklike snow is the color of your skin, the blue crocus, the color of your eyes. The yellow summer sun, the color of your voice, and the autumn rusts and reds, the auburn of your radiant hair. Love always, your daughter Laurie." It always makes me cry when I read that. That's my Mum. She could never find the way to be her own person, but what she couldn't do for herself, she was able to do for me.

I'm definitely a feminist, in recent years growing more and more militant. *The Maleus Malificorum*, the Christian handbook for ferreting out witches, says: "When you allow a woman to think alone, she will always think evil." The basis for witch-hunting was that a woman's brain cannot be good. And the basis of Christianity is the temptation of Adam by Eve with the apple of the forbidden tree. What is that? The apple is the sacred symbol of the witch. My feminism is not the kind that demeans men, because our religion honors men and women equally. In the old times, both women and men were warriors, lawyers, healers, managers of the money, rulers of the tribes. But in the modern world, the balance has shifted radically. The situation of modern women is worse, far worse, than in ancient times. As women, we need to recover our self-reliance, the source of which is in the mind, where all magic resides. By taking time to meditate, to touch earth with our bare feet, to learn our connection to the phases of the moon and the turning of the earth, we can use our psychic powers to project goodness into the world, always remembering that everything good that we do comes back to us threefold. We can project for a better job, a safer environment, a keener sense of relationship, economic stability, self-love, courage, freedom. The collective power of women's magical projections can heal the world.

It's very hard for any Druid to see what society has done to rape and devastate the earth. We are like lemmings, committing suicide by overpopulation, destroying the forests, polluting the sacred waters and the air. The Grail story illustrates this perfectly. The story of the Grail is a Celtic legend that was taken over by the Christians. The Grail is the beautiful golden cup of the goddess, representing the womb. The cup is filled with the waters of life, the gift of the goddess. The legend says when a king ignores the goddess, the land will fail him and the earth will die. Today, we have kings everywhere who are ignoring the goddess, the feminine side of nature. The world is horribly out of balance, wars are raging, people are clamoring for air, for space, for food. But Mother Nature will compensate and find the balance, through plagues like AIDS, if necessary, through famine, drought, war. The earth needs time to heal, and will take the time to do it, whether we humans wish it or not.

Life goes on in many forms. That young man standing next to his mother was as real as you or me. In the Druid religion, when you walk into the spirit world, you can see everybody you loved who died. Which brings the knowledge that the spirit is a continuous entity, that nothing is lost, no energy is lost. Looking at the transformations of nature, the caterpillar into the butterfly, the phases of the moon, the rotating of the earth on its axis and the changing of the seasons, I know I'm exactly like everything in the universe, which has a season that will come to an end. But it's all still glorious. I'm going somewhere, not ending anything. In fact, at this stage of my life, I feel more than ever a sense of youth, of rebirth. I'm sixty-three years old and the author of three books, but about to take a creative writing course at Salem State College. I'm taking up painting again, which I haven't done since my twenties. I've chosen to spend the rest of my life with the golden goblet and the chalice of the goddess, to put all the passion of my sensual, sexual self into my work, which I finally understand is to spread the word about witchcraft, and help the magic work its way into the world.

THE WISDOM
OF THE BODY

∽ *Marion Woodman, 65* ∾

Marion Woodman, a well-known Jungian analyst, international lecturer, and workshop leader, was born in a small town in Canada and worked as a schoolteacher for twenty-five years before beginning her training at the Jung Institute in Zurich, Switzerland. She is a specialist in dream interpretation and eating disorders and has written several books and produced audiotapes on addictions, dreams, the power of metaphor, and the creative process. She lives in London, Ontario, with her husband, a retired college professor.

I had the gift of faith, right from the beginning. My father was a minister, and our house was right next door to the church. As a tiny child, I used to go every day to the church and communicate with what I called "angels." I would hide under the pews and wait for God, hoping to catch a glimpse of Him while He wasn't watching. My father kept a magnificent garden behind the house, which was where I really lived. God was the spirit behind that garden, the spirit of life and death, as manifested in that garden. Or I would play in the graveyard nearby, and have tea parties and great conversations with visitors who would come with their flowers and talk to me about their husbands, wives, and children who were buried there. It didn't seem in the least strange or macabre to me. In the graveyard, as in the garden, I found the spirit of death and life, the spirit I've always called "God," by which I mean the Divine Feminine as well as the Divine Masculine. But it doesn't matter what it's called. That spirit is not a dogma, not necessarily connected to traditional religion. For me, it's the energy that changes and transforms whatever it touches. And my faith in that divine spirit has stayed with me always, right up to the present day.

My childhood prepared me for my life. I grew up in a small town in Canada where everybody knew everybody else and respected the individual, no matter how eccentric. As a result, I accepted my own eccentricity, my own uniqueness and aloneness, in a way that later helped me discover my own solitary path through life. Until I reached the age of six, I was a very happy, imaginative, fiercely intuitive child, living the life of my soul. But after the age of six, I began to hide my soul's truth, feeling that no one really understood me.

I had always been a kind of Cassandra, saying exactly what I perceived. But after I entered school, I began to see that my perceptions were not acceptable to other people, particularly my teachers, who were nervous about what I was going to say next. I was big, I was loud, with *huge* energy. That could cause a commotion in the classroom. In any case, I was absolutely attacked by my teachers and classmates for being so different, for not obeying the laws. It wasn't that I didn't want to obey the laws, it was just that I had my own ideas about how to do things, like cooking and sewing, and I didn't understand why it was necessary to do them the teacher's way. The home economics teacher became totally fed up with me and banished me from her class. Even though I loved cooking, I spent my entire time in cooking class on top of a ladder, cleaning and recleaning all the venetian blinds in the classroom. The irony was that I was trying desperately to please my teachers. I would do what they told me so exactly that they thought I was parodying them. And then I *really* got it, and never understood why. So I learned to keep my mouth shut, to hide my real self, which lived in my books at home, in the church, and in the garden. At school, I was in hiding. No one knew who I really was.

It was when I was in high school that I discovered a passion for dancing. I believed in creative work as a means of developing my relationship with God, which was just the hottest fire I could get into. Through dancing, I could achieve a state of illumination, go higher and higher into spirit, into a state of such electrification that my body forgot that it needed food. Saints have known this for centuries, that if you want to go deeply into the world of the spirit, you fast. Eventually, of course, I had to face the fact that my anorexia was a denial of the body, an illness, and that caused me to question my whole definition of God. This God that I was worshiping was obviously going to take me to the other world, and I wasn't ready for that yet. But that realization didn't occur until I had been anorexic for almost fifteen years.

By the time I got to high school, I literally stopped talking. Whenever I tried to speak, the words would come out in a whisper, or get caught, strangled, in my throat. In school, I seemed to get into deeper and deeper trouble. I would go home and read the poems of Emily Dickinson, who alone seemed to know the isolation I experienced. She was my dearest friend. Her poetry articulated what nobody, absolutely *nobody*, understood in me. So I would read her poetry out loud to myself, and that kept me sane, because there was at least one person who understood. But in the world outside my bedroom, I was still hiding what was most sacred to me.

In my fourth year of high school, my loneliness suddenly improved tremendously. One day, I was sitting in the back of the room, very quiet, trying, as usual, not to attract any attention. Suddenly everyone was staring at me, not with their usual indifference or scorn, but with respect. Because I had gotten a ninety-eight in Latin. That was the turning point. It was as if I was suddenly illuminated. I began to get high marks in everything, and for the first time was accepted by my teachers and the other students who were used to getting ninety-eights. My last year, I was elected president of the student council. For the first time, I felt that there was a place for me in the world. The life that I had been secretly working on at home suddenly connected with other people.

While training to become an English teacher, I went through another period where I was unable to speak. I was supposed to be teaching poetry, but the poetry meant too much to me, was too close to the bone. I could speak for about two minutes, then suddenly my voice simply refused to come out. All that terror I had experienced in the classroom came back. My master teacher, an old army colonel, a man of great sensitivity, allowed me to work with composition and grammar, and by the end of the year, I was able to come back to the poetry. Thank God he understood what was wrong with me, because he made it possible for me to teach, and I was born to teach.

I didn't get married until the age of thirty, to a professor of English at a university in London, Ontario. He was the most intuitive man I had ever known, with a luminosity about him that attracted me intensely. There was a fire, instantly. But I didn't particularly want to get married. I wanted *freedom*. At the end of teacher training, I had this sense of finally being let out of school, like a kid at recess. I wanted the *passion* of life, wanted to know how it felt to really *live*. I was so anxious to see the world, to be with people, to find the great art treasures of Italy and to follow the paths of the poets in England. So off I went with my rucksack on my back, youth-hosteling around Europe with my new friends. I had planned to stay for only a year but ended up staying over two years. I started out in England, traveling through the Lake District, but while there, I thought, Well, might as well go to Ireland, might as well go to Finland, to France, to Italy, to Spain. . . . I loved the life of a gypsy, getting up in the morning and not knowing what was going to happen that day or where I was going to sleep that night. And yet I knew that marriage was also somehow part of my destiny. So two years after returning from Europe, I married my husband.

From the beginning, we both agreed to follow our individual paths. Solitary, but parallel. We each give immense strength to the other, but we don't lean on each other. It was a true marriage, a marriage of two souls, as we found out through the barriers we encountered in subsequent years. My anorexia prevented me from having children. I always had a secret soul life—my anorexia was part of that—always thinking of the body as a sacred vessel, the temple for the Holy Spirit. I didn't yet recognize that *soul and body are one*. Outwardly, I fit into a predesigned social pattern—the university professor's wife, the schoolteacher. I dressed like a teacher and had my hair cut as a teacher, and apparently was nothing more than the good, respectable, responsible woman in the town. I adored teaching and loved my husband, but something was pushing me out of that world. In 1968, I traveled to India by myself, searching again for that heightened sense of spirit that had always been expressed for me in dancing, in not eating. And it was in India that I finally learned to accept my own body for the first time.

I became very, very sick in India, almost dead from what I had done to my body. Alone at the Ashoka Hotel, I fainted. When I came to, I was no longer *in my body*: I was on the ceiling, looking down at it breathing in and out, waiting for my spirit to come back. My first reaction was that it was just a stupid creature lying there, didn't know it was dead. But then I suddenly felt immense compassion for this "thing" breathing on the floor. There was a sweetness about it that reminded me of my dog, just waiting patiently and helplessly for me to return. I had the choice either to go back into my body or leave, permanently. So I came back in, and never again turned away from it.

God turned me around in that hotel room in India. I couldn't have done it without grace. It was as if some divine being just picked me up by the scruff of the neck and said, "No, not that way, Marion, *this* way." I understand now that every time the Divine has intersected my human path, it has been through my body. Huge transformations always take place in moving through these blocks. From that time on, I was able to see the wisdom, the sweetness, the fun, the *forgiveness* in the body. If you're living in the body, you have to forgive. As long as you are out of balance, living too much in the spirit—anorexic, idealistic, expecting perfection of everyone, including yourself—you are neglecting the wisdom of the body, which teaches you how to love yourself, and therefore love other people. Caught in the spirit alone, the *heart* is neglected, compassion, self-acceptance, self-forgiveness are neglected. The pain of coming back into my body has been immense, for me, and it's still going on. But that is what has taught me love.

I had gone to India looking for a guru, but I was too sick to find one. Instead, two years later, I found a wonderful Jungian analyst, and he became my guru. In analysis, my full maturity began to emerge, and for the second time in my life (the first was from infancy to age six), I relearned how to speak in my own voice and allow my own personal truth to emerge. That certainly had a radical impact on my marriage. My husband knew me as a quiet, gentle person. Now, he had to contend with this entirely new creature, this much more honest, forthright person, with a new energy and passion, a new connection to her soul. It's hard to accommodate change in a relationship, to accept that the person who's emerging is not the person you married. But if the marriage is a true marriage, one where destiny is at work . . . when that destiny is recognized, and you do love each other, that love can bring you through the hottest fires of hell, and take you through to genuine relationship, to a deeper love for the reality of each other. And that is indeed what happened. He was able to find his own energy, the passion within himself, which could meet what was emerging in me. It was a lonely search, for him as much as for me, because it's something you can only do for yourself, by yourself. But because of that effort of his, and mine, the marriage was able to continue, even stronger, now, than before.

This process of rediscovering and expressing my true voice is an ongoing one—beginning from the age of six and continuing to this day. It's only quite recently that I have somehow found the courage again, the courage I had in childhood, to say what I think, to be who I am, no matter how crazy that looks sometimes, and to speak my truth. The soul grows, even as it's speaking. It feels like a blossom that's been in bud for fifty years, then suddenly the light shines warm and it can unfold. But that didn't happen, for me, until rather recently—perhaps the last ten years or so, when I was well into my fifties.

I believe that much of my guidance throughout life has come through dreams, and that God is the dream maker. So whenever I get one of those *big dreams*, the kind that wakes me up, symbolically and literally, the kind that changes my life around, I pay attention. In my last year of teaching, I had a dream in which I heard these words: "Turn your face toward Jerusalem and don't turn back." I knew that Jerusalem was, for me, Zurich, Switzerland, where the Jungian Institute is. I loved teaching school, didn't particularly want to be an analyst, and certainly didn't want to leave my home, my husband, my school and students to go to Zurich for five years. But when I kept having that dream, with the voice telling me to turn my face to Jerusalem, I realized I had to go. Sometimes you fall into patterns, and your life isn't growing fast enough, there isn't enough being demanded of you. That's the situation I was in before I had that dream. So I had to open up into something totally new, like the poems I had been analyzing all my life. A dream is like a poem. It centers on one image, which develops symbolically throughout the dream. In analyzing poetry, I was quite used to the symbolic world, so relating to dreams was also natural to me. And my dreams kept forcing me to change my life, kept forcing me in the direction of Europe.

When I was in Zurich, I got word that my mother had had a heart attack. On the airplane flying home to be with her, I had another one of those *big dreams*, a dream that changed my whole feeling about the Feminine. It brought me into a sense of sisterhood with my mother that I had never experienced before—a sisterhood that opened up into my relationships with all women. I experienced the feeling, in my dream, of being not just a woman but *Woman*, and my mother being *Woman*, and coming from a line of *Women*, going all the way back to the Stone Age, and all the way forward into the future, where at last we could function as equals to men. After that dream, I somehow knew that women *are* equal to men, which caused me to change entirely my huge projection about men, that they were the authority figures, the powerful ones, rather than human beings, stumbling like everybody else. I had always looked up to men. I had lost my voice in the presence of the authority figure, the male. And, putting masculine spirit on such a pedestal that I couldn't even eat, had almost allowed spirit to destroy my body. I had all that, in spades. And then to be able to experience the beauty of being *Woman* was huge.

In 1979, I returned home as a Jungian analyst, in deep debt. When I failed to get a practice going in my hometown of London, Ontario, I began to wonder if I had done the wrong thing, had misunderstood the message of the dream. Then, after being home five months, I went to Toronto, saw this office, and had a dream that night, saying, "Where doors are open, walk through." So I set up my office in Toronto, and have been working here for the last fifteen years. My husband stayed in London; he had tenure at the university and his world is there. I've been coming home on weekends and commuting to Toronto during the week. Summers, we go to our summer home together. It's been a wonderful, enlightening experience. But now that phase is over. I'm in God's country again. I don't know exactly where I'm going or what form my work's going to take. Because a year ago, I was diagnosed with cancer.

It is one thing to know that you will die. It is another to experience the terror *in the body* of being extinguished. After all those years of denying my body, and then to wake up in the night and feel the burning fear of *this body* not existing in *this realm* anymore, makes me see and smell and hear and feel in an entirely different way. I have never seen the colors of the tulips so red, almost too red to endure their own redness. The baby leaves, all different colors of green, the chickadees . . . How magnificent this earth really is, and how sad that this beauty will not continue forever. It's sad that we don't recognize so many things until they're over, or nearly so. That is why I'm so grateful for this illness. To have a chance to look at everything a second time is huge. *Huge.* I have been acutely aware of life regenerating itself, and of myself being resurrected this spring. I think that comes from a new realization of the miracle of my own body—not only its going into the descent of illness, but the miracle of how it can regenerate itself, how wise it is and how exquisitely beautiful, even if it is *old*. It has a beauty that is luminous.

When my friends learned that I was ill, I got many suggestions about what I should do—all given in love. What clinics to go to, what diets, what natural doctors, as opposed to traditional doctors, meditative exercises, voice exercises, journaling . . . I received so many books and tapes and recommendations that I got lost in a kind of daze of confusion and began to think, "Well, there's no straight line through here at all, I'm probably going to die." Although I valued every suggestion as part of the golden net that was supporting my very life, there came a point when I knew I had to take responsibility for it—my own healing—myself. I had done a lot of bodywork in my clinical practice, so I was able to move into conscious witness and dialogue with my own body, hear its wisdom, what it wanted to eat, when it needed rest, when it didn't want to or couldn't take the radiation treatments anymore. Eventually, I was able to act out of my body's wisdom and find my own path through that forest.

To me, the wisdom of the body means finding out what the *soul* wants, as opposed to the ego. Ego focuses on order, control, the known and the knowable, the life that I have understood. Taken to a terrible, inhuman extreme, that is what anorexia is. An anorexic does not recognize the wisdom of the body, only the laws of perfection, which are basically technological laws. Going against our human instincts amounts to a nasty sense of perfection, which will kill every human trait, if necessary, to get what it wants. Food addictions hit women more than men, because we are more connected to our bodies in terms of the monthly cycle, childbearing, and so on. But men suffer just as much. How many men have forgotten the wisdom of the body? How many are workaholics, technocrats, walking machines, who will probably fall dead, eventually, of a heart attack? What's a heart attack? The heart finally decides it's going to feel something, even if it's only grief.

The world we have created, in our culture, is essentially an addicted world. Addicted to control, to power, to materialism. The addiction dictates the lie that the more "matter" we accumulate, the happier we'll be. But then the human being inside goes crazy and says, "Well, if you've got power, I'll have power, too. I will eat and drink and have drugs and have sex, everything I want, I will have." Rather than surrendering to the mystery of the soul, to the Divine that exists in all of us, we try to reach our god or goddess through more *money*, more *sex*, more *chocolate*, more *perfectionism*. This is the opposite of surrender to God. Because the feminine spirit has got to be recognized. She will kill you if you don't.

I really think, now, that this is my true path, the path of *soul*. Much of my work has been with women; women seem particularly susceptible to judgmentalism and condemnation of their bodies. We really must learn to forgive our imperfections, to accept our human limitations, to accept ourselves as we are. Not to try to impose order on the universe, but to be strong enough to surrender to its mystery. There is no sense of order on the path I'm on now, in fact there is total chaos—God's country, the country of mystery. I know I'm dealing with a treacherous disease, and I don't know what the future holds, but right now, I have come through to what seems like a luminous place, a place of sublime beauty. I feel that I have come out of death into new life.

FORGED IN FIRE

∽ *Ai Ja Lee, 55* ∾

*Dr. Ai Ja Lee is a prominent acupuncturist and herbologist of Korean descent
who was born in Peking, China, and immigrated to the United States in
1974. She has been practicing acupuncture, traditional Chinese medicine,
and Western pharmacology for over thirty years, first in Seoul, Korea, and
then in New York City. Her expertise in Oriental medicine has led to a
second career as a lecturer and consultant, instructing Western doctors on the
practice of acupuncture and herbs, and researching and lecturing on the possibilities of helping AIDS patients through ancient Chinese healing techniques.
She is the mother of three daughters and the grandmother of two, and currently
lives with the family of her second daughter, Serena, in New Jersey.*

Youth is a square: It has sharp edges, it gravitates toward extremes, it goes in one direction toward a goal, then turns a corner and goes in another direction. In youth, we cultivate the *mind*. The mind is wonderful, but it's not everything. Old age is a circle: It includes everything, it contains heart and spirit, its edges are smoothed down by experience, like waves on a shore. I had a good education, and thought I was pretty smart. But smartness is not wisdom. Wisdom is walking in somebody else's shoes, understanding how human it is to feel ashamed, to be afraid. So bad, sad experiences are good for people. They give you more humanity and sensitivity to other people in pain.

When my mother was growing up in Korea, there was a saying: "There are three ways of life for a woman. When young, always obey the father. After marriage, obey the husband. When the children grow up, follow the son." Traditional women were not allowed to go to school, own their own business, or protest if their husbands had a mistress. She married a man she loved very much, but she believed in the traditional way: The man walks ahead, the woman behind.

During the Japanese Occupation of Korea, my parents fled to China, where I was born. Then, when the Japanese occupied China, too, we moved back to Korea in April of 1945. When the war ended and our country became independent, the Japanese took everyone's money out of the banks and nobody ever saw it again. My father died that same year. Then my mother, who had taught herself to read and write even though she never went to school, had to start all over again. She did beautiful hand sewing, not machine sewing. She saved the money she earned and opened a little restaurant, which became very successful. Since women couldn't own their own businesses and she wanted to expand the restaurant, she married again, when I was seven.

At first, my stepfather didn't like me too much. Western civilization had touched our country after the war, so by then girls were allowed to go to school. Since my grades were very high, I started to get more affection from him—he was proud of me. Girls had to compete with boys by taking entrance exams to go to junior high school, to senior high school, to college. I usually won first prize in these examinations. In high school, the teachers would give us pages from the Christian Bible as an exercise to improve memory. But I read those pages, and that made me think maybe someone is up there, maybe God is up there. My country's national religion is Buddhism, but Buddhism does not have a single omnipotent God, a Creator. I started going to church and became the chairman of the youth organization of the YWCA. One of the church leaders asked me to become more political, to give speeches to bring more people into the church, but I said no. My religion was for personal enrichment, not for politics. I do not like politicians; most of them are liars. I wanted to make my soul deeper, not give speeches. I was searching for God, and that was private, not public.

I was in my second year of pharmacy school when my mother died. I didn't understand why my stepfather did what he did next. After fifteen days, he had a new wife. Now I see why he married so fast. It's because he did not know how to read or write. He needed someone to maintain the estate, the property, and the business. So he married a woman he hardly knew, a bad woman who stole from him. There was a lawsuit, and she went to jail for stealing, which shocked my stepfather so much that he had a stroke and became paralyzed. The medical system couldn't help him, so I invited an acupuncturist to the house to try to heal him. After only two months of treatment, his drooping cheeks were suddenly lifted up; he could walk. I saw how my stepfather was healed, and thought, "Oh, there's something in this." So I went and learned acupuncture.

In pharmacy school, I was honored by one of my professors, who wanted to give me a scholarship to study surgery. But I had two younger half-sisters—one was very sick with polio. I said, "No, I have to take care of my sister." My professor was angry at me. "Anyone can take care of your sister, but not everyone is smart enough to become a surgeon." I said, "No, she needs me." So I gave up the scholarship and took care of my two sisters while I finished pharmacy school, which at that time taught herbal medicine along with Western pharmacology. Then I was able to practice my herbal medicine and my acupuncture, traveling to remote villages and tiny islands where there was no medical care, to give children innoculations. I never regretted giving up the scholarship, because today my sisters always say, "She was not our sister, she was our little mommy." Human beings are more important than careers.

After graduation, I married a pharmacy school classmate, and we had three daughters. He worked for a private company, and I had a private healing practice. My patients were the ones the hospital sent home to die when there was nothing more to be done for them. My name became known in the community as a healer. I think my husband had a problem with my success: He felt *smaller* than me, not as smart. I said, "Why aren't you proud of yourself for having a smart wife? You can't be a stupid man if you have a smart wife." But he always felt *less*: inferior. I learned that he had a girlfriend. When I confronted him about it, he hit me. That shocked and shamed me. After twelve years of marriage, he wanted to get divorced. In Korea, if there is a divorce, the husband gets the children and all the property. I said, "No divorce. I want to keep my babies." We fought about this for a long time; we were always fighting. Then one day he suggested that we emigrate to America. I did not want to start all over again in a new country. "I can never be a real American," I said. "I could go to America and eat bread and butter, but I could never have blue eyes and blond hair." But then I thought, "I better go with him, because if he wants to divorce me in America, I can keep my babies."

We moved to New York because that was the only state that would allow us to take our pharmacy exams without going to school first. My husband took the exam three times and failed. I passed the first time. That made him even more angry than before, more violent. I told him, "This is America. If you hit me once more, I'm calling the police." I never thought he was a bad man—just frightened, and feeling inferior to his wife, which hurt his pride. So he left, taking the car and the furniture and all the money with him. I had three dollars left, and three babies to support. I was so ashamed to be left this way, without being able to speak English or earn a living yet or support my children, that I thought seriously about committing suicide. Then I sat down down and made a list of reasons to live. The most important reason was that if I died, I would not only be killing myself, but I'd also be killing my daughters. I wrote on the list that I had a gift for helping to heal people, to give them hope. I wrote that I still had my health. These were all powerful reasons to live, even though I had equally powerful feelings of depression. But I don't think, if I had not had that desperation, that shame, that I would be the person I am today.

Hard experiences make you less arrogant. I couldn't have understood my patients' agony as well as I do now, unless I had gone through my own agony. Knowledge is not enough. Knowledge is factual. One plus one equals two—that's knowledge. But experience tells us that one plus one can also equal three or five. Life is hard, and just knowing facts doesn't help much in getting through life.

After my husband left, I worked as a technician for a man who made costume jewelry. Too proud to work in a factory, and desperate to support my babies, I worked twenty hours a day. Maybe in a week, I would sleep three or four nights. Even the wholesaler was surprised; he said, "You are doing the work of five people. Go home and go to sleep." But I couldn't—I was too desperate. Jewelry artists make a pattern first, then they melt the metal in fire, then pound it and pound it until it is flat, then etch it with sharp instruments in order to make a beautiful design. I thought that I was going through the same process that it takes to make jewelry: I was going through fire, getting pounded by fate. Many times in my life, I went through fire, but the result was not always the way I wanted it. Then I thought that evidently God thought that more fire was necessary, more pounding, more etching with sharp tools. We endure what we have to, in order to make the beautiful design of our lives.

It took three years before I could get licensed as an acupuncturist in New York State; meanwhile, I went back to school for a Ph.D. in Oriental medicine. I started teaching acupuncture to licensed acupuncturists and Western medical doctors, who began sending me their most difficult patients, those who could not be healed by modern methods. I was interviewed on television and quoted in magazines. Soon my reputation became established and my business bloomed. I bought an office building in New York, a condominium in New Jersey, and some land in Florida. I bought a Mercedes. All these *things* made me feel like a success. Then again, in 1991, disaster hit. There were two fires, two months apart, in my office building. It was insured, but it took months for the insurance to pay. Meanwhile, I had borrowed money at high interest to repair the building, but when the second fire happened, I couldn't pay the mortgage; I couldn't repay the high-interest debt. I had to declare bankruptcy.

That was the darkest, lowest point in my life—even worse

than when my husband left. Before, I was ashamed because of being abandoned by my husband; this time, my shame was something I caused myself, by taking that high-interest loan. My reputation, my practice, everything I owned was lost. I really didn't think I had the strength to start all over again. It was only much later that I was able to understand that the fire, the pounding made me stronger, made the metal stronger, because it deepened my faith in God.

The process of life, from youth to middle age to old age to death, is to create something beautiful—the soul. In youth, we are like a flower blooming in the greenhouse. We don't know the world. We haven't experienced pain yet. We haven't felt the wind, the rain, the snows burying us in winter, the miraculous rebirth of spring. In age, we turn into wildflowers; we feel the power of nature, the hardships but also the beauty in life. The butterflies land on us, the bees search for food. That helps show us our place in the universe—to be useful in some way, to serve somehow, to give a gift. We are all a part of nature, and everything in nature has a purpose. I would rather be the unknown, even unnamed wildflower blooming in the woods than the most beautiful orchid decorating some wealthy person's living room. And now, when horrible things happen, I tell myself that I have more strength, more guts, because I am the wildflower, in harmony with nature, and not the hothouse flower protected from life.

Human beings are very flexible. We have the power to bounce back again and again, both physically and psychologically, from terrible trauma. It all originates in the mind. Sadness and pain can weaken the spirit, but if we have a happy, strong mind, we have the power to resist invading viruses. Positive thinking can work miracles. Sometimes we think, "This is the end," and give up. But it doesn't have to be the end. The world is a mirror: You reflect good into it, and it reflects good back at you. An unkind, selfish, greedy person will have his selfishness reflected back at him. One of my patients is a very wealthy woman in her forties who was in a deep depression, worrying about losing her beauty, worrying that her husband might leave her. I said, "Dear, why are you crying? You're so beautiful, you have everything. Think of what you have, instead of what you have not." I thought that the more she cried about her husband leaving her, the more reason he would have to leave her! The mind is a powerful tool. It can create your destiny for good or for evil. So we might as well train it to help us, not harm us.

There is a balance in everything. Without balance, our health suffers. Greed for money can destroy our health. Yes, we all need a certain amount of money to live, but not as much as people think. How much is enough? We need a car, but do we need a Rolls-Royce? We need a house, but do we need two houses, five houses? Work and play—balance. Cut down a tree, plant a tree—balance. If you keep watering one plant in the garden, it becomes rotten. We must circulate the water, circulate the wealth, share with other others. That promotes health of the body, the spirit, the community, even the world.

I am an American citizen, but in my heart I am Korean. When my children were young, I used to tell them every day, "Never forget your roots." Because without roots, we are not anchored, we just float like a cloud. I have a dream that after retirement I will move to a small village in Korea where they have no doctors, where all my education and knowledge can be used for helping people in need. I dream of this all the time— going back to look for a place where I can be of service before I die. America is a wonderful place of enormous opportunity, but it has no respect for the elderly. Old people are put in nursing homes, so no one will have to look at death. Western civilization throws its old people away; it has no humility; it is ruled by ego; it thinks it needs a lot of money to be happy.

After the bankruptcy, I learned how little I really need. I really believe that serving other people is the solution to the problem of old age. Human relationships come and go, and money goes down the sewer. But giving help to other people never ends. Before all my bad luck came to me, I looked down my nose at people who were less fortunate than me. Now I wear their shoes.

SHE WHOSE
VOICE RIDES ON
THE WIND

∽ Grandmother Twylah Nitsch, 83 ∽

Grandmother Twylah is a spiritual elder in the Wolf Clan of the Seneca Tribe in upstate New York. Born on the Cattaraugus Indian Reservation, home of the Senecas, she has been a teacher and lecturer on the teachings of Native American people since she was nine years old. After graduating from South Park High School in Buffalo, New York, and dropping out of college during the Depression, she was hired as a recreational supervisor for Erie County, where she worked for fifteen years. She has traveled widely as a lecturer in Europe and across the United States and is the author of four books on the mythology and philosophy of Native Americans. Her husband of fifty years died in 1980. She has four children and four grandchildren.

We should never say *try*. We should say *trust*. Trust means that whatever work you are aspiring toward will be done well, with power and conviction and *energy* behind it. If you are standing in the middle of a big river, "trying" is like placing a big boulder in the middle of the river; it stops the energy flow in midstream. Only *trust* will keep the energy going forward.

When I was a child, I was told by my elders, my two grandparents who raised me, that the most important thing was to recognize my own truth. As long as I knew what the truth was, my dignity, my integrity, and my stability would always be assured. When I was little, I was a handful, always getting into things, but nobody ever hit me. *Ever.* The first thing the elders would say was, "Are you happy?" And I would stop and think and listen to my truth within. If I said yes, they would say, "Maybe you should think again. Maybe you can't see ahead to how you might get hurt." Getting hurt meant that there could be some kind of pain, the pain I could cause myself by not knowing my truth. So I was warned: If I continued, I would be solely responsible for the consequences—the pain—that would follow. That is how I learned the difference between right and wrong: Right is comfort, wrong is pain.

In Native culture, children are regarded as teachers, because they have not yet had any experience of having their truth and their trust chipped away by people who want to control them. Elders are also honored as teachers, because they have already performed their duties of learning and working and raising families, and what they have learned it is their responsibility and honor to teach. But when I was five years old, the government said that it was time for me to go to school, away from the reservation and into the home of a white family. That was my first look at the discrepancies between the two cultures.

In the home of the first family I lived with, there was a little girl my own age who was constantly being spanked by her mother. This mother was *huge*, and she was always hitting her child for something that was not very important, or for something that was the mother's own fault. There was very little discipline and almost no consistency in the house, so that it was hard to know what was acceptable and what would be punished. One day, she grabbed her daughter by the ear, yanked her down over her knee, and started hitting her. I went right up to her and said, "Stop! You're hurting your little girl!" At first, I couldn't understand why there was always so much yelling and screaming going on in that house. Afterward, I understood that this mother had no balance, no self-direction, because she didn't know what she wanted from one minute to the next. And it seemed to me that the reason was that she was not centered, she did not have an inner truth that she could depend on.

I also learned about competitiveness and jealousy from living in that house. The little girl disliked me from the beginning, because she was forced to share her bed with me. I knew immediately that I was in her space, and that it would be natural for her to resent me. I tried to stay as quiet as I could, so she wouldn't have any reason to resent me. Her parents forced her to take piano lessons, which she absolutely hated with a passion. I would listen to her practice, and taught myself how to play by ear. One day, her parents asked us both to play for their guests. I tried to refuse, but they insisted. And because the little girl hated the piano, she played badly, and because I loved it, I played from my heart. After that day, she never liked me. I tried to make her my friend. I told her I would never again play the piano, and that was doing a good job, and anyway, if we were friends it wouldn't matter so much. But she rejected my apologies and refused to ever walk to school with me again or be my friend. I saw that there would never be any possibility of friendship between us, because there was no *wholeness* in that culture, everyone being in competition with each other, rather than in *cooperation*, as I had been taught. So the culture was not compatible to either of us.

At school, I was different from all the other children. I didn't talk like them, didn't gossip, didn't giggle, didn't chatter; I never said anything unless I had something to say. I felt that some of the teachers were only interested in getting their paychecks at the end of the week, that they were not committed to teaching, but just to putting in their time. They would promise us many things, like a trip to the zoo, then not keep their word. I was very puzzled by that. Where I came from, people never made a promise they couldn't keep.

The second family I lived with loved me and accepted me as if I were their own daughter. The four boys in the family were just like the brothers I never had—kind, gentle, and sensitive. I saw them hurt and misused at various times—being lied to, promised a reward for work they had done that never materialized, being stood up by a friend—and that hurt *me*, too. Native people are taught that male energy is protective and female energy is nourishing and that we have both male and female capacities within ourselves. When the boys were hurt, I saw that males were just as susceptible to getting their feelings hurt as girls. The lesson there was, again, the value of truth: Dignity and self-esteem suffer when children are lied to. And because I loved them, I took on their suffering just as if it were my own.

Every summer, I would go back home and relearn the lessons of my elders: respect, self-respect, truth. Many people talk about how much they love their children, but few know what love really is. This society is bent on destroying self-esteem within its children. Children are deprived of the love and comfort they need when they're told they don't know anything, they're stupid, they're unworthy of being treated with respect. That can make them doubt their own truth. All children are born knowing what their truth is, but that can be compromised when people are constantly lying to you. It can change that posture of trust that we were born to have toward life. Trust is the thought, love is the action, and truth is the source.

Living in the homes of white families during the school year was a huge culture shock to me. The lesson was that not all people live alike, not everyone thinks alike. I knew I would be rubbing elbows with all kinds of people all through my life and that I had to learn to get along with even incompatible people and look for the truth within each person. If I saw examples of meanness, lying, disrespect, lack of integrity, I realized that they were not living their truth, and therefore had all kinds of lessons to learn. Whenever I encountered such people, I used to write a tiny mark on the steps of their house that nobody could see except me. If I made a mark in orange crayon, it meant that they didn't keep promises. A pencil mark meant that they had poor judgment and lacked integrity. Pink meant they lacked compassion. A circle meant that they were whole, complete, but a straight line meant they had a long way to go. I was learning about all these other people, deciding whether or not I wanted to be their friend. I decided that it was up to me to be available if they wanted to be friends but that it didn't affect *my* truth in any way if they didn't. Later, I was ashamed that I had defaced the entrances of their homes and went around and rubbed them off.

In Native culture, children are given names before they are born. When my mother was pregnant with me, my mother was told by her father that she would have a little girl, that the girl would be fragile, and that her name would be Yehwehnod, which means "She Whose Voice Rides on the Wind." It would be my destiny, my grandfather said, to live that name.

There is an ancient story that was handed down through the generations to my elders. There were four people of wisdom—one deaf, one sightless, one crippled, and one forgetful—who used to sit together all the time. One day, there was a total eclipse of the sun, the world became dark, and the people were very frightened. A hand appeared in the sky, and a voice thundered down, saying, "See this hand, four fingers and a thumb, when the hand is closed, all fingers become united, the hand becomes one." When the four people of wisdom heard the message, they came as teachers to our people to teach this lesson of unity—that the necessity for growth sometimes requires going deaf before we can hear, blind before we can see, crippled before we can move, and forgetful before we can remember. So before I was born, my destiny was given to me: I knew that my physical body was fragile and that I would have to learn my lessons through the frailty of my body. My grandfather said that before my voice could be heard in the world, I had to experience the loss of my senses and then regain them in order to see, hear, and move in the right direction.

When I was still in high school, I lost my hearing for eight months. Because I couldn't hear anything, I wasn't distracted by noise or chatter. I began to write poetry, because I wasn't only *listening* to my inner truth, I was able to *hear* it much better. My deafness introduced me to my spirit teachers, who speak in poetry form. Spirit teachers need this sort of communication to make a connection with human beings on earth. Each teacher expresses a particular rhythm; thus the need for rhyming. Years later—I can't remember exactly how many years because time loses its meaning when you can't see the clock—I went blind. It was wonderful being blind. It gave me a measure of awareness into the dimensions of time, space, distance, the shape and weight of the world, that I wouldn't have had otherwise. The lesson in blindness is that you have to *see*, not just look. When you're blind, all of your other senses are heightened and magnified, which increases your sensitivity to the living world, to its beauty and perfection. Anyone can do it, we can all get into that dimension, if we choose. All we have to do is close our eyes and focus on our truth within.

I'm having trouble with my eyes now, but I have no fear of blindness, because I've been there. I'm grateful that I have seen trees, I have seen my family, my friends, the mountains, the sun and the moon—I've seen everything. I don't have to feel that I am being deprived of seeing nature. Everyone has to go through some darkness sometime, but if you've already experienced blindness, it holds no unexpected terror, the terror of the unknown. Eyesight is a bonus.

I learned very, very young, even before I went to live with white people, about the cycles that women go through—from childhood to procreation to old age to death—and that this cycle was natural, and therefore sacred. There is only one time in life set aside for producing children, and only one mate for that purpose. I knew that sex was sacred, because it's part of a natural function of bodies, and you don't play around with anything that's natural. I had a reputation in high school of being untouchable—the boys used to say I had a cement wall around me. I loved to go out, have fun, and dance, but sex was sacred and limited to one true mate, and I hadn't found him yet. When I did find him, I married him right away. We went to live in my ancestral home, in the same house my mother and I were born in. He was a wonderful person of Dutch descent, and his mother put him, her only child, out of her life because he had married an "Indian." He often said that my mother and dad were more parents to him than his own. We had four children, two girls and two boys, and right after my last child was born, I became a cripple.

The doctors had given me a spinal block for anesthesia during the delivery, and there was some kind of injury to my spinal cord. I went completely numb in my legs and feet. For three years, I couldn't walk. I had to find alternate ways to move—a wheelchair, crawling on the floor, pulling my body behind me like a frog. . . . Because it was my destiny to teach people how to heal themselves, and my students would be people with multiple disabilities, and I needed to understand where they were coming from. I felt, in my own body, what it was like to be crippled, and was grateful for the opportunity to become more aware, more sensitive, and more compassionate toward other cripples. That was the lesson I was supposed to learn. Every time I lost something, I never asked, "Why is this happening to me?" I asked, "What can I learn from this?" My grandfather had told my mother that I would overcome all these handicaps, so I *trusted* that I would. And I did.

I was raised both in my own culture's religion and in Christianity, and I have no quarrel with any religion one chooses to embrace. I had fun with all the churches I went to, and as far as Jesus Christ is concerned, I think he was a good man who got a lousy deal, being hung up on the cross like that. The main drawback I saw to Christianity was that every time, as a Christian, you summon up the image of God, it is always a male image, and my culture raises us to understand that the Supreme Being contains both male and female energy. The worst thing that happens to humankind is when the *truth within* is taken away and put out on a cloud somewhere *out there*. Then people who are looking for God start looking in the wrong place, because God is and always was and forever will be within. *Separation* rather than unity, and *control* rather than freedom, became the way the word of God was disseminated. Western cultures seem to want to divide everything into light and dark, good and evil, the right way and the wrong way. They do not realize that everything is light, we are all beings of light. We have no darkness within us, we have *lessons* within us. Blackness is listening and thinking, harmony; there is nothing more harmonious than black. When the Western cultures accuse somebody of being evil, they are blinder than I was when I lost my vision. Turn *evil* around and it spells *live*.

My husband and I raised four children and were very happy together for fifty years. Just before he died in my arms, I said to him, "Oh, please don't go yet, Bob," and then I remembered something that had happened when I was seven years old. I was home for the summer, and one morning I was awakened by a huge bump, as if something heavy had been dropped on my bed. I opened my eyes and saw a gigantic rat staring at me. The rat looked into my eyes and I looked into his eyes, and something happened to both of us in that moment. It sounds ridiculous, but I saw the truth of his being in the eyes of that rat, and he saw the truth in mine. *Love* was exchanged between us. Then the cat jumped up onto the bed and started mauling the rat. The two of them were fighting, screeching, making horrible noises. I ran downstairs to call my grandparents, and when we all got back upstairs, the cat and the rat lay dead on the floor in a pool of blood. I was horrified. We buried them together in one box, in a deep hole in the backyard. My grandmother said, "This is good, burying their bodies together. They have finished their work and learned their lessons, and now they're going back to the earth where they came from." After that, I was never again afraid of death. I saw the very, very thin line that separates life and death, that they are two parts of the same whole, the vital energy that can never and will never be lost. So when Bob was dying and I begged him not to go, I said, "No, I can't say that to you. You've finished your work, and that's wonderful! You certainly can go, and we'll talk later on." I rejoiced that I had the chance to know him, to be with him for fifty years, and felt the peace that comes from acceptance and gratitude for being allowed to take this earthwalk with him, even though his life was now coming to an end. And that gave me so much comfort, knowing that everything was exactly as it was supposed to be, that life and death are exactly as they are supposed to be. So I wasn't miserable that he was gone, but happy that his work was done. I didn't emphasize the horror of his dying; I emphasized the release, the learning. Because death is an experience that we all have to learn. And I knew I would see him again when my earthwalk was over. There is no death, just a change into a different dimension.

Before he died, my grandfather, reminding me of my destiny, said to me, "You will continue where I leave off. Your voice will appear in the world." He said it was time to start writing down the teachings so that they wouldn't get lost. I vaguely recall making a promise to him that I would do what he asked. Then, just before my mother died, she sat down next to me in the kitchen and said, "I'm getting tired. I've taught you everything I know, and now it's time for you to carry on." She walked to the sink and threw her blood pressure pills down the drain. We spent the next twelve days talking, and then on the twelfth day, she took the hearing aids out of her ears, and died a few hours later, at the age of eighty-five. I was living within the white society and had forgotten the teachings. I was very busy, working as a teacher and raising my children with my husband and constantly running around all the time. I had decided, years ago, that I didn't want my voice to be heard in the world. I felt that no one was really listening, anyway. It seemed to me that most people thought they knew everything already, and therefore their eyes and ears were closed to the truth. And so I began to feel that what I had to say wasn't important.

As a child living within the white society, I was considered slightly abnormal, because I was always foretelling things that made people uncomfortable. I was constantly told to be quiet, not to talk about "stuff like that." When I was alone in my room, in silence and in stillness, I would hear voices talking to me in poetry. I knew that these voices were not *mine*, not consciously, but they matched the deep truth within that I recognized as my own. Although I felt these images powerfully, I never wrote them down, except during that one period in high school when I lost my hearing. Later, I shut the voices out completely, feeling that my ability to discern the difference between lies and truth might be misused. I was fighting my destiny; I needed to be writing, but I didn't want to write. So when I was already in my seventies, the first thing that happened was that my dear old friend who I hadn't seen in years came to visit me, and when I saw his face, I was so happy to see him that I hugged him, and he hugged me so hard, he broke two of my ribs. Everyone in the room heard the noise of my ribs cracking. Then a week later, I fell and fractured my kneecap. Before that, I was still running around doing things, not writing, but when I broke my knee, my destiny spoke out, saying, "You have not been responsible, you have not been disciplined, you must now sit down and do nothing but write." So I was forced to stay in the house and begin writing down the teachings. I don't really care anymore whether it sounds good or is acceptable to people; I'm just writing because it's my responsibility to do so. And I think that it's not just my own destiny but the destiny of everyone, somehow, some way, to make their voice, their inner truth, heard in the world.

A lot of people are running around these days calling themselves healers, but no one is a healer. How can anyone feel someone else's pain? Only the sick person knows what his inner truth is. Healing is attracting truth, and truth can only move through silence. So when someone is sick, we teach them to be silent, to listen to their truth within. If they don't know their own inner truth, there are guidelines to help them heal themselves, to awaken their awareness of what they can do for themselves. People sometimes call me a healer, but that is not an accurate description of what I do. I teach people to give thanks. Not to pray, because prayer is asking for a favor. In giving thanks, we ask for nothing for ourselves, because everything we need is already here, provided by Mother Earth. The trees are growing, the rivers are flowing . . . Everything is as it should be. Healing means gratitude—gratitude for being allowed to perform this earthwalk, to be given the gifts of Mother Earth, knowing they're walking *with* the earth, not *on* her. Healing is being grateful for being allowed to survive. In one's own nature is the clue, the key to healing, and that key is gratitude, the source of which is truth.

SIMPLE ACTS OF

KINDNESS

∽ Matilda Raffa Cuomo, 63 ∾

Matilda Raffa Cuomo, the former First Lady of New York State, was born in Brooklyn to a large, close Italian immigrant family. Married at the age of twenty-two to former Governor Mario Cuomo, she worked as an elementary-school teacher before their five children were born. Mrs. Cuomo has been an activist on issues relating to children and families. As First Lady, she was the chief spokesperson for the Governor's New York State "Decade of the Child" and the founder of the New York State Mentoring Program, a school-based K-8 program that links adult volunteers with at-risk schoolchildren. In 1995, under the auspices of HELP (Housing for the Less Privileged), she established MENTORING USA, which extends the mentoring program nationally and includes the children of homeless families. Governor and Mrs. Cuomo now live on New York's East Side.

It all begins at the beginning. I came from the kind of Italian immigrant family that not only believed but *lived* the American dream. We were poor, but we all felt rich—rich in enjoyment, rich in love. We ate well, even though now, come to think of it, I don't remember much meat. I remember ceci beans and lentils, pasta with broccoli, a little bit of chicken, and a lot of vegetables. But we couldn't afford meat. My mother was a scrupulous, frugal shopper who would walk over a mile to the farmer's market, saving a few pennies by comparison shopping, going from cart to cart picking out produce, my hand in her pocket so I wouldn't get cold. Both my parents worked incredibly hard. My mother, like every other mother from that culture and that generation, did the cooking, the cleaning, the laundry, and the darning of the socks, the complete raising of the children. My father, who had been a master carpenter in Italy, worked in New York City as a carpenter to support the family. He thought America was the greatest country in the world. "In this country, you can reach for the stars," he'd say. "Nothing will hold you back, except God."

My father later became successful in business, but he never forgot the early hardships, which I always felt had strengthened rather than embittered him. He told the story of being driven to work in the open cabin of a truck in midwinter. His two bosses wouldn't let him sit inside the truck. It was snowing; he almost froze to death. From the back of the truck, he could hear the two men arguing, one of them saying, "What do you think he is, a dog?" My father heard them say the word *dog* several times, and for a long time he thought that was his English name. Years later, after he had built up his own business, one of those fellows came to him asking for a job. Without even giving it a second thought, he hired him. I think that story perfectly epitomizes my father's character—his goodness, his kindness and decency.

I always admired and respected my parents, but now, as a grandmother, I can appreciate even more how difficult it was for them. They couldn't speak English very well. When my mother brought me to public school to enroll me in kindergarten, her lack of English was a terrible embarrassment to her. The principal didn't understand what she was trying to say, so he asked her to leave. I'll never forget my mother's trauma, her humiliation that day! I held her hand, and all the way home she was gripping it and crying. That experience had a powerful effect on me. Somehow it caused me to withdraw into myself. I was a shy, quiet child. I didn't really come out of myself until the sixth grade, when I was lucky enough to find a wonderful teacher who helped me overcome my shyness.

I decided to become a teacher because of Miss Conway. I remember everything about her—her pure white hair with a bunch of curls on both sides of her head, her sweetness, her compassion, her quiet demeanor; I don't think there's a child in that class who will ever forget her. My habit was to run home from school, then tell my mother to come to the front door while Miss Conway was walking past so we could wave to her. The thrill of my life was when she let me be her clothes monitor! I thought I'd died and gone to heaven because I could hang up Miss Conway's clothes and keep them tidy in her closet. She made me feel special, like I was *somebody*. Somehow, she singled me out for special attention—letting me be her clothes monitor, waving to me, and turning around like that, with that sweet smile, recognizing me. And on Parents' Day, when my mother was unable to come to school because she couldn't speak English, she took especially good care of me. I wanted to be exactly like her.

Apart from my shyness outside the house, I had a rich, full family life—not just the immediate family, but cousins, nephews, aunts, in-laws. We'd go on big family outings to public parks or to Coney Island in my father's big open truck, singing "Roll Out the Barrel." Baby-sitters didn't exist in those days. My parents never spent money on the movies or went anywhere without the children. The world has changed so much since then, with the mobility of families spread out all across the country, the disappearance of the extended family. In those days, we didn't stray. Even when we got married, it was terrible to move away from your parents, even a few towns over, like from Brooklyn to Long Island. I could never have met my husband, who was from Queens, if I hadn't gone to St. John's Teacher's College. I lived in Brooklyn and never dated any boy from Queens—that was too far away. I know it's old-fashioned, and nobody lives like that anymore, but maybe a little more old-fashioned attention to the family is just what the modern world needs most.

I really blossomed in high school. Midwood High was an experimental school. The students elected their own officers—a mayor, a treasurer, a controller, and a police force. The way you distinguished yourself at school was to get elected to office. I started as a guard, checking everybody out as they came through the exit; nobody could cut school or they'd get detention. And advancing through the ranks, I became an inspector, a supervisor, and an assistant captain. Then, another thrill of my life, they voted me captain! It was a revelation, a shy girl coming out of her shell. My father encouraged me to go out with lots of different boys, saying, "Matilda, how else will you know what to look for in a fellow you may someday want to marry?" He trusted me absolutely, but always wanted to meet my dates. When, in college, I met my husband, I took him home to meet my parents. As soon as she met him, my mother said, "He's a good, sincere boy, Matilda. He'll never hurt you." I asked her,

"How can you know that? You've just met him." "I can see it in his eyes," she said. Just about a year later, he came to my father and formally asked for my hand in marriage—very traditional, very old-school. After a very short whirlwind court-ship, we were married. My mother had enormous intuitive power; she still admires my husband today for his integrity and compassion. We just celebrated our forty-first anniversary last June.

I had been hired as a teacher in my senior year in college and got married right after graduation. When I came back from my honeymoon, the principal said, "You're not the woman I hired. You've got a new name, and you're pregnant." I taught the second grade until my ninth month of pregnancy, which was a scary time for me, because I knew very little about childbirth. I knew it was going to be painful, because my best friend's mother called me and said, "Matilda, do you know what labor is? Labor means pain, honey. And you're going to feel pain." It's a good thing somebody told me *that*. My mother's generation wasn't open to discussing sex, so I was completely ignorant, completely unprepared. I didn't even know *how* the baby was going to be born. I had a wonderful female doctor who kept consoling me all through the labor, telling me that what I was feeling was *normal* and that I would live through it. But I couldn't believe how much it hurt! And when they gave me anesthesia, I thought I was never going to wake up. But the minute my daughter was born, I regretted *nothing*. Even if my religion didn't forbid birth control, I would have had ten, twelve kids, if they had come.

Many young women have asked me, "Why didn't you go back to school and get your master's? Why did you allow"— *allow*?—"your husband to work his way up in his profession but not pay any attention to your own career?" I told them, "Because I chose to stay home with my children." Many of my friends had returned to school to work on their master's, so I did think about it a few times. But I tell you, with all my heart, the minute my children were born, I loved them so fiercely that I wanted to stay home and be with them. To mold these kids, to help them develop, to bring out their strong points and strengthen their weak points, to have family dinners together, to watch them grow—I couldn't think of any accomplishment that could have been more wonderful or satisfying for me. The children were the pot of gold at the end of the rainbow. They made even the hardships all worthwhile.

It's so sad to think about what so many young kids are going through today. In New York State alone, there are 63,000 children in foster care; 500,000 across the country. These kids represent families who have broken up. Sometimes I go to residential centers to talk to the boys and girls there, and I ask them, "What is troubling you so much? How did you get here?" They tell me, "What is this 'love' you're always talking about? I never had any of that." They don't understand what it is to get a sincere hug. They never had anyone coming to them and saying, "Hey, you've got to go to school, because I love you and you're worth it and are going to become somebody." Nobody ever told them, "I believe in you, so you have a reason to believe in yourself." If the mother is hardly ever home, if she's drinking or taking drugs, if she has a boyfriend who treats her badly, how is that mother going to mother her own children, when nobody ever told *her*, "I believe in you"? Many of the boys in prison were locked out of their own homes; they didn't even have a place to go to the bathroom! All children start out beautiful and innocent. Then, usually around the fourth or fifth grade, trouble starts happening to them because they're so unhappy. Would *you* be happy if you weren't treated right? So because they're lost, unloved, that's how they become felons when they grow up—because no one ever showed them a single act of kindness.

No matter how many religious people you study—St.

Thomas Aquinas, Aristotle, Buddha, Christ, Maimonides—their message was always the same: *Love one another.* I'm so saddened by the racial hatred that's tearing this country apart, families disintegrating, children having babies. . . . I can't understand how we can make so much technological progress, going to the moon, inventing new and better weapons of war, while losing sight of the *basics*—the principles that I was brought up with and tried to teach my children: to honor your parents, cherish your children, care for your neighbors, respect even strangers, not do anything mean . . . It doesn't matter what faith or religion you are, *we must believe in something.* When times get tough, and they will—we all have tears to shed—you have to believe in something in order to avoid the seductions, the temptations, the easy solutions—drugs, sex, violence. To me, loving means understanding, relating, remembering, respecting, and appreciating the differences among us. We all know what is the right thing to do. We know that love and respect are good, and hatred and cruelty are bad, but it's not enough just to *know* it. We have an obligation to teach it to our children, and not just with our words, but with our actions. Acts of kindness are the best legacy we can hand down to our children.

In the beginning, when my husband was secretary of state, becoming involved in politics was a difficult proposition for me. Public disclosure and the public eye used to make me very uncomfortable. But when my husband was campaigning for election, I was asked to make some campaign speeches for him. I've often thought of how hard it must have been for Eleanor Roosevelt, a teacher, a private person, with an unsteady speaking voice, to give speeches for her husband. I read that Roosevelt's campaign manager told her that her husband would not win unless she campaigned for him, that she had to keep his name alive. The idea that I had to go and speak in public was completely terrifying to me. But the way I made it more bearable was to prepare a lesson plan about his achievements and why people should vote for him. That was easy, because I absolutely believed every one of those reasons. And eventually, every time I spoke in public, it got easier and easier.

A lot of my personal growth took place after all the kids were in school. My fifth and last child was born when I was just forty. When Christopher reached the third grade, I went back to work as a substitute teacher. After my husband was elected governor, my first thought was to teach in the small school that was right next door to the Executive Mansion. Instead, he asked me to chair his Council on Children and Families. At first, I balked. I worried about how my being away during the day would affect the children. Also, I wasn't sure if I was really qualified for the job. My husband said, "You're the mother of five children. You know what parenting is all about. You're also a teacher. That's a perfect combination to find out what families need." So I agreed. I didn't know where to start, so I started from scratch, using not so much intelligence as intuition, the common sense I had learned from my parents. There was a huge bureaucracy in place, and I had to learn to adapt, to listen, and get along with all the commissioners and directors. You can't get to first base without this foundation of genuine personal interest. At first, they were a little suspicious of me. Now they are all my friends.

When Christopher left home for college, I felt suddenly alone. I couldn't stand to go into the family room, where we had always had our private time, and not see him there. I was tearful quite a few nights. The books say that after your children grow up, you feel an emptiness because you're not needed anymore. I had always felt that all the kids needed me—to see them off to school in the morning, be there when they returned, feed them, take them to their ball games, their dance lessons. They always had so much to tell me after school. . . . Every time I thought about it, I got weepy. It was a hard lesson for me, to start a new phase of my life, to come to the realization that I belonged to myself, that I now had time that was mine alone and could do with it what I wanted. That new freedom wasn't too easy for me. For a long time I was a little stuck on the idea of dependence. But as my children have matured, I've learned about a new concept: interdependence. The people I love still need my support, my counsel, and I always make them my priority. Even with my new lease on life, the family still comes first. I go to visit my ninety-year-old mother once a week. When my daughter Maria had a baby, my son-in-law was surprised when I stayed two weeks to help them with the baby. I said, "Kenneth, it makes me feel good that I'm needed here and can serve a purpose here for you." Maria and Margaret, my oldest daughter, could have had a nanny, but they wanted their mother, which I thought, and still think, was wonderful. I wouldn't have traded it for all the honors and awards in the world. First things first.

Sometimes I still get sad at the fact that the kids don't live at home anymore, but I believe that keeping yourself busy is the cure for loneliness. And coming into this whole new world, and traveling—to South Africa, to Spain, to the Republic of Malta, where I launched the UN Year of the Family, giving commencement speeches and becoming involved in the Decade of the Child—these have been years of highly satisfying work for me. As an advocate for children, I try to help them stay in school, not get pregnant, and fulfill their potential. If they don't get support, guidance, and discipline at home, then they need a mentor. They need *somebody* to give them hope. That's why I started the New York State Mentoring Program. I have mentored two children. One of them could very well have become an eighth-grader with a baby. But because I interceded when she was in the *fifth* grade, she now has a future. Her grades have improved; she wants to be a lawyer. She's in her third year at Albany High School. She has a nice boyfriend now, a real jock on the football team, a good boy, I did some investigating.

When we go out for lunch, I still sometimes worry a little about her and her relationship, but she tells me not to worry, she's got better plans for her life than getting pregnant.

Women have progressed so far forward in my lifetime. One of my daughters is a doctor, another a lawyer, another the chairman of HELP, the largest national provider of housing for homeless families. . . . There's nothing standing in the way, today, of women rising to whatever station in life they choose. Women deserve to be and to do anything they want, but once we have children, we have to remember we're mothers *first*. First things first. Even while we're struggling to survive with our professions, we have to make all kinds of accommodations, because those children are our responsibility. Their survival depends on us.

The basic values I was given as a child have continued to grow. There's a real thread of permanence when you have a solid foundation at the beginning, which stays with you always. Centuries ago, the matriarchal cultures came about because of the strength of women, because they bear the babies and raise them. A woman has to be stronger than a man. Balancing work with family is always difficult; women can become stressed out, stretched too thin, trying to meet too many obligations. Single mothers have an especially hard time. In Sweden, the government sends in helpers early to assist these young mothers. That's what we tried to do in New York State—provide at-home assistance and early intervention *before* families break up, to catch the plague in time, before the kids become felons.

Why are all these programs needed? Because so many family members give up on each other. Husbands and wives who must have loved each other once are simply too immature to deal with the problems that will always come up in a family. Times get tough, there are economic problems, arguments, distractions; he's working too hard, she feels neglected, they both feel unappreciated. Young couples give up too quickly. They're looking for a perfect situation, but there *is* no perfect situation. We're all so different! No two people are alike. We bring our own baggage to a relationship. We're absorbed with ourselves. So when the little problems come up, they can turn immediately into catastrophes, because the concept of sacrifice is out of fashion these days. Young people who marry at seventeen are too immature to say to each other, "We love and respect each other, it's worth it, what we have is worth saving. Let's try harder." Instead, they want it all, and they want it *right now.* Well, that's not going to happen. So they give up, and the children are the casualties and victims of their immaturity.

In my work, I never stray far from issues concerning children and families. Except for breast cancer. I've lost too many close friends to this horrible disease. With all the reputation women have earned for speaking out, we still haven't quite learned how to advocate effectively for ourselves. We suffer silently. We don't complain enough. When Jack Kennedy wanted to get funding to land on the moon, he brought all the separate space agencies together and created NASA. That's what we have to do with women's issues, like breast cancer, which have traditionally been given lower priority. Why cancer is any less important than going to the moon, I have no idea. I can't stand it; every time I think about it, I want to cry. The only thing I can do is volunteer my time and work as hard as I can to help bring coalitions of cancer groups together and promote education for the prevention of breast cancer. In unity there is strength.

Recently, I met an old friend at an awards dinner. She said, "I want to know who does your hair, where you go for your face, how you stay looking so young." I said to her, "Listen, I'll tell you the truth, I'm too busy to to worry about how I look or scrutinize myself." The only time I look in the mirror is to fix my hair and get some makeup on. I would say to any woman who is feeling depressed, or over the hill, or not needed anymore, "Don't stay home and watch the TV. Get dressed, go out, volunteer. The whole world needs you! Call any community organization to give anything you have to give, even if it's just a smile, a word of encouragement to somebody." I really believe that volunteerism is the cure for every negative emotion—boredom, loneliness, unhappiness. Busyness takes away the pain. And think of all the positive things you can create by helping just one person lead a better life. A simple act of kindness can change the world.

THE GOOD GENERAL

✿ Sally Jessy Raphael, 52 ✿

Sally Jessy Raphael is one of the most respected and popular television talk-show hosts in the United States. A veteran of over thirty-nine years in the broadcasting business, she was born in Easton, Pennsylvania, and grew up in San Juan, Puerto Rico, where her father worked in the rum business. Her broadcasting career began at the age of thirteen, when she hosted the "Junior High School News" in White Plains, New York. She then held numerous positions in the industry, including radio disc jockey and television news anchor. As a news correspondent for the Associated Press, she spent a great portion of her early career in Mexico and Paris. The Sally Show was launched in 1983; it airs in two hundred markets across the United States, in addition to the United Kingdom, Canada, Australia, Saudi Arabia, and Thailand. She currently lives with her second husband of thirty-two years, Karl Soderlund, and their brood of seven children—some biological, some adopted, and some officially foster—in Westchester County and New York City.

I was a shy child. I read everything I could get my hands on, had few friends and almost no dates. Nobody ever told me I was beautiful, so the fact that I wasn't pretty became nothing more than a fact of life to me. I always knew that character and brains were the important things, but of course, of *course* it hurt that I wasn't the kind of woman that men desired, that boys asked to the prom, that young men took home to meet their mothers. I was president of my junior high class, but I wasn't asked to the big junior high dance. I don't believe that I ever had a date in either high school or college. But somehow, making a virtue of necessity, I went out very early and started working at thirteen years old, aiming for a successful life according to my own definition of success. I'm a communicator, I've always been a communicator, and I decided early on that I would try to make the kind of living that would allow me to communicate with numbers of people in a way that made a difference in someone's life. And, defining success in my own terms in my own way, that definition never included being gorgeous or making huge sums of money or becoming a celebrity.

It took twenty-six years in this business before I ever earned a salary of over twenty thousand dollars a year. I was fired eighteen times throughout my working life. Each time I was fired, I indulged myself in a few days of self-pity and then immediately got on with the business of getting the next job, and then the next. I always knew who I was, always had friends and people who loved me and whom I loved. If your identity is completely and solely wrapped up in what you do and how much you make, you're already in trouble, because these things are temporary; even careers and fame and money are temporary and come to an end.

I used to think that when I got old (old was about forty to me then), I would get myself *fast* out of America and move to Europe, to Italy or France, where the culture seems to appreciate older women more. Once, in my twenties, I went to a cocktail party in Italy and noticed that all the men were looking at and talking to an older woman, attractive, certainly, but well into her forties. It struck me that that would not have happened in the culture I grew up in. This society treasures new, young, dewy faces with very little history behind them. This is particularly true in the business I'm in. The only older woman in an anchor position I can think of in the United States is Anne Bishop, now retired, in Miami. I used to joke that whenever an anchorwoman reached the age of thirty-five, they would take her out into the alley behind the studio and shoot her, while letting the male anchors grow wonderfully old and craggy. Where do these aging anchorwomen *go*? It's really not fair that just when a woman is getting to the point of an impressive resumé, where she's covered conferences and been a foreign correspondent, somebody lets her go for a young blonde from Vassar without that richness of background and experience. We really should require that whoever takes this experienced newswoman's place as anchor should have at least as good a resumé as the one she replaces. We should demand the same background from women as from men, and not worry about how they look.

Ever since I passed my fiftieth birthday, I've realized that my priorities have changed. I ask for quality from each and every minute I'm spending now. Before, a day was a day to get through. Now, it's a day to be savored, no matter what happens. It has to be a day of communicating about something meaningful (not just chat), of taking away pain from someone else, spreading any kind of generosity or goodness so as to lighten the burden of somebody. When I know people are in trouble, I call them much more often than I used to. I don't use the excuse of "I don't have time." And I make sure to touch base with the people I dearly love at least once a day.

I'm no stranger to death. I've lost a child, my parents, and many friends. And that caused me to investigate and to come to terms with it. Because I've made it such a project, to learn everything I can about what I'm most frightened of, I've lost my fear of death. Once I was in an airplane that was crashing and I was amazed that I felt absolutely no fear or palpitations at the time. Fascinated and deeply curious, yes, but not afraid. Not that I have a particularly religious view of life, or that I think there's a world beyond. On the contrary. I just think that death is a natural part of life and when it happens, that's the way it's going to be and the way it's supposed to be.

I've learned how to study things that I'm most afraid of, to make the fear go away. As a child and teenager, I was consumed by many fears, mainly physical ones. I was afraid of the water, so I would never go swimming. I was afraid of playground slides, afraid of hurting myself physically. For a long, long time, I was petrified of the dark, afraid that it would engulf me completely. So I trained myself to face my fears. I put on a snorkel and a mask and, scared out of my wits, got down there and did it. Once, I was watching a group of nine-year-old boys going down an enormous slide, and I just jumped right on and slid down! Then I forced myself to walk into dark rooms and feel my way around until I understood that there was nothing in that room to fear. You have to be familiar with the enemy, to know what the enemy's next move is, if you want to be a good general.

Whenever I get troubled about something, I always try to discipline myself to get up off my knees and stop whimpering. It's terribly important at every age to somehow leap out of the constriction of one's own mind and get involved in something larger than oneself. Do whatever you want to do. Write a poem, plant a rosebush, go to India, be kind to other people. And of course, as our government is shutting down more and more, we rely more and more on individuals to do the work of the world. For God's sake, I say, find your place and your cause and something besides yourself to get passionate about. Go out and make the world work. Take any one thing that needs to be done in the world and add one little bit to it, and that will pay off immeasurably, mostly in terms of helping yourself.

I know that someday I will stop this very satisfying work that I'm doing and go on to other things. I'll read a ton of books, I'll travel—very, very slowly, without an itinerary or time schedule—to see the cultures and the animals that are fast disappearing from the earth. My mother was an accomplished painter, and two years ago, I, too, began painting. My path has always been to communicate and to facilitate, but you can communicate with a paintbrush, too.

RESIGNING AS GOD

❧ Gretchen Woods, 50 ❧

Before her call to the ministry at the age of thirty-six, Gretchen Woods was a music teacher while she and her husband raised two sons and a foster daughter. After obtaining a master's degree in religious studies, she began her first ministry in the Pacific Northwest, where she earned a doctor of ministry degree from Northwest Theological Union. In 1987, she separated from her husband, and in 1992, she moved to her current ministry at the Unitarian Universalist Church of Reston, Virginia. A highly nontraditional minister, she uses many different religious disciplines—Native American, Buddhism, Hinduism—in her preaching of religion and spirituality.

For many years while I was growing up, I bought into the whole idea of what a woman was supposed to be, even though, like an ill-fitting dress, that role never particularly suited me. My mother, who had been an incredibly gifted actress before she gave it up to raise a family, used to say, "A woman is the dirt under a man's feet," then elaborated on that by saying, "She's the soil from which he builds his dreams." My father, who was more supportive of my personal ambitions and in many ways my safety, withdrew his support when I expressed my desire to become a physician, a surgeon. He said that I would end up getting married and not using the education, and suggested nursing instead. But I wouldn't co-opt myself that way—my one small rebellion, outwardly at least. But inwardly, I was filled with conflicts, confusions. My energy, my intensity, made a lot of people uncomfortable—I was called various things, like "intimidating," "ball-breaker," which was not at all what I was about. In college, I studied music, which I loved but had almost no gift for. I couldn't sing in tune and was what they called "rhythmic-defective." Six days after my graduation, I got married to a man who thought I was a free spirit, an independent, ambitious sort of person. But almost from the minute we got married, I turned into my mother.

I did everything my mother did—tried to be a buffer for my husband, the "soil for his dreams." We had two sons, moved several times for his job—he was a mechanical engineer—and with my degree in music education, I gave music lessons at home, very, very modestly, and sang in a chorale. When my sons were eight and six, we adopted a fourteen-year-old foster child, who became very important to my journey—a highly gifted, strong-willed child with a history of rebellion against authority. She was constantly challenging my long-held assumptions about what a woman was supposed to do and be in the world. She felt that being *only* a wife, a mother, the soil under a man's feet was not enough. She made me apply the lessons I was constantly teaching her to my *own* life, and that process caused a slow but inexorable change in me.

For instance, I was always encouraging her, as much as my sons, to make the most of her brains and ability, to study and work hard at creating something of value in the world. But she was always saying, "What about *your* talents? Why, if you think that what a woman brings into the world is important, why are you making it secondary to your husband and children? If you think that each one of us has an important gift, why are you burying *yours*?" At the time, I was writing poetry in secret, poems I never tried or expected to get published. Her incessant theme was: Why is a woman expected to focus *all* her energies on other people rather than reserve at least a part of it for herself?

All of this came to a head during a two-week trip I took with my husband to Taiwan for a science conference. I was thirty-five, an age that was for me some kind of combination of delayed adolescence and early menopause. I had never rebelled from my family, as many young women do. I had never traveled out of the country before, except once to Canada. My husband was away all day, and what I learned was that I was able to get things done and get around quite well by myself, on my own, without the language of the country. Part of it was the natural honesty of the people there. I knew I could get into a cab and give them the fare and they would give me fair change. It was really quite simple, this matter of taking care of oneself, and I felt very comfortable and had a good time, to my own astonishment. That helped me somehow break free from the image of the limits of what a woman was supposed to be able to do.

I spent my thirty-fifth birthday sitting in the Grand Hotel, where I was supposed to be preparing for an upcoming recital. That's when I first realized it was time to decide what I wanted to do when I grew up. My kids were getting older and needed a different kind of nurturing from me—the difference between what I called "smothering and mothering." I thought about going back to school and finally getting a nursing degree, or a degree in social work, or that long-abandoned M.D. And then I looked at the stack of books I had brought with me—a book on Taoism, *Myth and Ritual in Christianity* by Alan Watts, a book on contemporary Buddhism, and Will Shutz's *Profound Simplicity*—and realized that what I really wanted to do to put together my intense interest in the intellectual life and my interest in how people interact and what their lives are about spiritually. So, after giving it much thought and meditation for about nine months, I went back to school to prepare to enter the ministry.

Meditation was an important tool in this process. I had given up meditating from the time my children were born until that time in Taiwan, age thirty-five. One of my sons was asthmatic, the other had nightmares, and I found that if one of the children needed me when I was into a deeply meditative state, I would stand up and get dizzy, almost black out, because I have low blood pressure. So I thought it was just easier to give it up. But I returned to it during the nine months after we returned home from Taiwan. It wasn't really a sense of calling, like God coming out of the clouds and saying, "You must go now," but a gradual clarification of what mattered most to me, a process of examining whatever skills and aptitudes I had and how best to manifest them in the world.

When it became clear to my husband that I was going to change my life, he changed his job to accommodate my new schedule. He was always very helpful, very supportive. I found the closest school, a large Roman Catholic university nearby. This particular religious studies program had students from many different faiths, not just Catholics. The department understood and accepted the denomination of Unitarian Universalism, with its pluralistic faith stance. We don't have any kind of dogma, doctrine, or creed. We all share in the search for God *together* and are not terribly uptight about the way religion is practiced, caring more about living our values in daily life. We practice, as well as preach, the inherent worth and dignity of every person, justice and compassion, acceptance of all people, encouraging spiritual growth in all people, the right of conscience, the inter-connectedness of all of life. There exists the perception that the Roman Catholic Church is conservative, patriarchal, not too welcoming of women who want to become clergy. But the Jesuits who taught me were very much high scholarship–oriented, intellectually curious, and open to new ideas. My experience was of being tremendously supported and mentored by my teachers. Of course, they did know that I was not planning to be working in the Roman Catholic Church, so that may have contributed to their unfailing support.

I managed to schedule my classes for the middle of the day and at night, in order to see the children off to school in the morning and be home for them after school. After graduation, I was called to a congregation in Washington State, and my husband again changed jobs to accommodate the move. Two of those years of that first ministry were a wonderful honeymoon. And then my husband decided he needed to leave the family.

Why does it take twenty years for a marriage to end, if it's supposed to end? I think it's because women are socialized for twenty years before they get married, and it probably has to take at least that long to unlearn the negative lessons. Women coming into their power are hard to be around.

I was one of those women who was hard to be around. I suddenly had many responsibilities outside the home. I was always busy, going to meetings, trying to take care of the needs of the congregation as well as my family. But my husband was a private person. A lot of public attention was focused on him that I don't think he particularly enjoyed. At the same time, I was also responding to questions my foster daughter had raised years before, issues of gender and sexuality, which helped me come to accept not that I am a lesbian, but that my sexuality is not particular to gender, that my responses have a great deal more to do with experiential connection than with plumbing. It's not about how this person looks but about what kind of energies I experience with them. And my husband became restless, and began searching for relationship with others.

Ministers and therapists are the biggest projection screens on earth. When my husband became involved with a member of the congregation, it was a very messy business. It was hard on my children, on me, on the congregation, and on my ministry. Preconsciously, I think, to some degree, the church had hired a family, rather than a minister. When we no longer fit that model, it was difficult and uncomfortable for some people. I did stay on for five more years, but felt that my work there had been compromised. When I received a call to ministry in Virginia, I moved back east. My former husband has remained a concerned, involved father, very attentive and supportive to the children.

I've been at this congregation in Virginia for almost two years. We're having a wonderful time. There are no divorces in my future. Two years ago, a woman with a great spiritual understanding moved in with me. She's not disappointed if I have to spend every evening out at a meeting, because she's deeply involved in her own work. There is no competition between us. We're compatible and happy together. All six of our children—my three and her three—call us "Moms." This relationship is just a joy in my life.

I don't call myself a feminist theologian, because my approach to religion, as well as to everything else, is more holistic. "Feminism" can be a limiting term: It doesn't include enough. I have two sons, for example, who are trying to bring their creative gifts out into the world for themselves and for social transformation, in some kind of collaborative way, but not for the purpose of accumulating lots of money and power over others. Some people would call this "feminist," but I disagree. I think the screwup is that we have confused masculine with "power over" and feminine with "power under," when the dichotomy should be, as Starhawk writes, "power over" versus "power from within." My sense now is that ministry is about spiritual midwifery—a call to authenticity. As a minister, I use *my* best power from within by encouraging my congregants' transformation, their self-birth. Every human being is a cocreator and gift of creation to the world. Our call is to determine who we are and what our particular aptitudes are, and how best to bring them cocreatively into the world. That call should be, in some way, from my perspective, midwifed by the church.

One of the saddest things about the way girls are socialized is that we are trained to believe that we can, or at least *should*, get power only through a man, thus becoming phobic about locating the source of our own *power within*. So much of education and socialization is about *managing* energy, rather than encouraging and releasing it—as my foster daughter used to say, "Children don't grow up, they grow *down*." We are all born with an incredible gift, a uniqueness, a force that sometimes makes society uncomfortable. So it tries to manage it, control it, categorize and label it, put it into boxes. Women intuit this, in some way, and back away from control, often giving away their power in order to avoid this inappropriate controlling. Or they may, in their power phobia, and feeling so out of control, try to covertly manipulate other people, rather than be up front about it, which is a really horrible manifestation of perverted or distorted power. Erich Fromm wrote about this in *Escape from Freedom*. In my own case, I respected the authority not only of mother and father and husband but of anyone who had more experience than I. I had learned to discount my own experience, my own thought, my own heart. Anne Wilson Schaef wrote that the choice to live makes a person unmanageable. The choice to die is the choice of the psychotic and the schizophrenic and the suicide. So society asks everyone to make the bargain *not to die and not to live*. But this is a very bad bargain. We must all choose *to live*.

Jung said that every psychological problem is really a spiritual problem. Each one of us has a unique spirit, a soul, with a point of contact with consciousness as such, which is what I call God, or the powers of the universe or whatever. I always encourage all people, male and female, who are struggling to make contact with the power of their soul to find a spiritual discipline. I don't give a damn what that discipline is: It could be Buddhist or Native American or Christian devotions or worry beads, we need an *intentional* process to open ourselves to that point of contact, to the spirit, an intentional way to create time for it to speak in our lives. My spiritual discipline is to start every morning praying the Native American medicine wheel, then go out into the woods, which makes every day start with a very earth-centered grounding. I also try to chant every day—obviously not when I'm in a board meeting—and that also provides another kind of grounding. In the Native American tradition, you intentionally pray, but then whatever your prayer is to any of the directions, you have to listen twice as long as you pray. So I believe it's very important to create enough time and space to get back into contact with God, or consciousness, or any other name you care to give it.

I've very much come to live that wonderful Zen saying, "Nothing that's urgent is important, nothing that's important is urgent." The only exception I can think of is a two-year-old with his finger in a wall socket—you definitely move on that one right away. My patience has increased with age, my ability to let some things go. Some things are never going to happen, I realize. We're human beings, we have limitations, we can never make everything perfect, in the Greek sense, but perfection in the Native American sense is possible—the sense of being wholly and authentically who one is. John Bradshaw says that the real human sin is not accepting one's human limitations. I was the first child of six and I set out to be the perfect child. The lesson I'm still working on is *resigning as God* and being clear about what I can and cannot do. Sometimes when I preach, other people take in a message that is far away from what I said or intended. Instead of reproaching myself for my failure to communicate, I understand that other people's misinterpretations come from their own filters. So I let it go. Sometimes, those misunderstandings can be a plus rather than a minus. I've had people say, "Oh, that was the most thrilling sermon, it helped me change my life!" And I'm thinking, "What did I say?"

There's a notion in quantum physics that a butterfly flapping its wings in China will affect the wind currents over the United States in time. That helps me to understand that while I'm flapping my wings here, I may not be able to make a great impact here and now, but that sometime, somewhere, it will have an effect. When I finished my dissertation and got it published, I gave a copy to each of my sons, expecting them not to read it for twenty-five or thirty years. A year and a half later, I got a phone call from my elder son saying, "I just finished reading your dissertation, I'm so excited, you're working in an absolutely original way, in a field that I'm interested in, and we've just gotta talk!" I was so thrilled to find that all that flapping did have some impact. I'm able to accept, now, that whatever is worth doing probably won't get done in my lifetime, but that's all right. Just so long as what I bring to it is the best I can.

The materialist approach to success is: "The one who dies with the most toys wins." My version is: "The one who dies with the most consciousness wins." Enlightenment means embracing the whole of consciousness, the consciousness within and beyond that rock, that flower, that river, the connectedness that informs and includes all of life. Charles Hartshorn talks about knowing a mountain as God knows it, not as a human measures its height, width, and the number of trees on it, but *feeling* the ants move through the soil, the trees' roots pushing deeply into the soil, the fire of the molten earth beneath. Seeing a mountain in this way can change your perspective forever. I know it has forever changed mine.

READINESS

∽ *Sandy Warshaw, 63* ∾

Sandy Warshaw is an activist in the women's movement and a fighter against discrimination in all its forms: sexism, ageism, racism. She worked for twenty-five years for the New York City Human Resources Administration, trying to make the bureaucracy more responsive to the community it serves. Since taking early retirement in 1992, she has been working full-time as an advocate for midlife and older women, and she has been a national board member of OWL (the Older Women's League) since 1990. In 1986, following a mugging and a beating, she became a student of Seido Karate, attaining her black belt at the age of sixty. The divorced mother of a son and a daughter, she lives in New York City.

When I was growing up in Scarsdale, I learned very early that there was a different value placed on boys and girls. Add to that being Jewish, and to that being Russian Jewish instead of German Jewish, and it all added up somehow to being lesser—a lesser person, of less value—than the children I grew up with, including my brother. And on top of that I was pretty competent in school and a little too athletic to please most people, which did not make for a prepossessing beginning of a young girl's life. When I went out on a date, my mother would say, "Be sweet. Don't argue. Don't let them know how smart you are." On the other hand, I was expected to get a good education at an Ivy League college—God knows why, I think it had something to do with increasing the status of one's parents. Although I did get an excellent education, that did not prevent me, by the end of my senior year, from feeling like a complete failure because I wasn't yet engaged, let alone married. There were all these idyllic pictures of Vassar coeds and their new husbands under the archway at West Point, and I felt, really, so left out and horrible because I wasn't anything like these lovely marriageable Vassar girls.

Shortly after my graduation, my father said to me, "Now that I've spent ten thousand dollars on your education, I guess the only chance for you to get a job is to go to secretarial school." So I took a speed-writing course that summer and found a job as secretary to the News and Public Affairs director at CBS. The speed-writing course got me an interview, but it was my religion major that helped me get the job. The network was doing a variety of programs on religion, then launched *Face the Nation*, with which I was able to help. But toward the end of my first year there, my father told me how worried he was that I was having too good a time working and might therefore never get married, like all my cousins and Scarsdale girlfriends. The thought of a career woman as daughter must have been just too horrible to contemplate. Since I loved my father very much, I married the first eligible man who asked me, quit my job, and immediately started having babies, which made my parents very happy.

During the early years of my marriage, when I was doing a lot of volunteer work at my children's schools and the local school district, I was invited to give a speech in response to a major school reorganization report. I accepted with some trepidation, since I had never given a speech before. I was thrilled when the audience seemed to respond positively to what I had to say. But after it was over, my husband was furious because I had been introduced as Sandy Warshaw rather than as Mrs. Milton Warshaw. He said, "I don't know whether that means we're divorced or I'm dead." That sort of thing seemed outrageously important at the time. I saw the handwriting on the wall.

I was ultimately hired by the New York City Human Resources Administration, which, in 1968, was equating volunteer experience with paid work. And thus started a kind of schizophrenia in which I was a serious, contributing member of the workforce from nine to five and the "little woman" at home. My husband didn't exactly forbid me to work, but merely made it difficult to do so, assuming—not maliciously, but simply as so many husbands do—that the house would be as smooth-running as before, dinner on time, his clients and coworkers entertained at home, and so forth. To keep up with the demands, I was taking medically prescribed tranquilizers, drinking too much, and smoking three and a half packs of cigarettes a day, and all of this initiated a sequence of events that ended not only my marriage but very nearly my life.

The turning point happened just after my forty-third birthday. I began to take a sharp look at the so-called life I was leading, or the life that was leading *me*. First, I checked myself into the Payne Whitney Clinic. While there, I learned I had breast cancer. After a mastectomy and nine months of chemotherapy, my marriage ended. Ten years after my mastectomy, I got mugged and beaten up. All of these things were a clarion call to me, an ultimatum: Either take care of yourself or die. I decided, despite all the psychic pain I was in, that I didn't want to die yet.

Now, looking back, I understand that I might not have been able to stay sober without the mastectomy and chemotherapy process. My younger sister had died at thirty-one, three years after *her* cancer was diagnosed, and I remember asking myself how I wanted to live if I had only three years left. That question, "How do you want to live?" became the theme of my life, the short time I then thought I had left. Sometimes it takes a near tragedy to help you ask yourself this terribly important question, perhaps the most important question there is.

That was the beginning of the change, the transformation— the desire and the determination to take myself seriously. After my marriage ended, I went back to school and got a degree in social work. My means of empowerment has always been to search out wonderful friends, people who believe in me, who help me believe in myself. It also strengthens me to become an activist in whatever area I need, privately, to get better at. For instance, terrified of cancer, I joined with some other women to start a group called SHARE, a breast cancer survival group. I found that activism helped me, at least as much as the women who joined the group, to stop thinking of myself as a victim of cancer. When I got mugged, a friend took me to a karate class, which helped me learn how to protect myself, instead of feeling vulnerable and powerless. Activism in the Older Women's League took me out of the role of victim of ageism to that of a person working to change the stereotypes and circumstances of older women in society. It's always a hell of a lot better to try to change a condition that needs it rather than suffer in silence. And even if my efforts don't bear fruit in my own lifetime, I can feel that at least I've planted a seed.

Lately, I've come to think of age as an adventure, a quest. I don't always know what I'm seeking, but I have a sense that something marvelous is waiting out there somewhere. I've begun to travel by myself, to Israel, Greece, Italy, to Yugoslavia, to England and Wales, and, this year, to Japan. It's lovely, if a little frightening, to make discoveries for oneself, to travel down a path with no particular destination, to stay with something intriguing and have no one else to answer to or negotiate with. Last year, in England, I promised myself: no museums, no cathedrals, no guided tours, just being there in a state of receptivity, of willingness to meet people and attentiveness to what was there. I brought no guidebook with me, only one dog-eared copy of *Jane Eyre*, and went to the moors in Yorkshire, where the Brontës wrote, and sat in the heather and scribbled in my journal and thought, I would never have been capable of this when I was younger. It was another test of my courage and strength—to see if I could do it, survive it, and thereby increase my confidence that I can do pretty much anything that pleases me.

Shortly after my husband and I separated, a friend said to me, "You're lucky. You live alone, your children are in college. Now you can do whatever you want to do." I thought, "What *I* want? What a quaint idea." I'd never actually asked myself that question. Without generalizing too much, I've noticed that many women are so used to defining themselves in relation to others—parents, husband, children—striving mightily to be the good daughter, the good wife, the good mother, that we forget, or possibly never learn, how to take care of ourselves. It can feel strange in later life, when one's responsibilities to others are diminishing, to have no one but oneself to nurture, and that is what is meant, I think, by the "empty nest syndrome." But I've found that one of the delights of getting older is sort of introducing yourself to yourself and trying to figure out what really moves you, what comforts you, what sets you on fire, what disgusts you, what drives you crazy. Back to that question again: How do I want to live with the time that's remaining to me? That, for me, has been *the* question of my later life.

I think what happened for many of my contemporaries, girls who grew up in the fifties, was that we had a concept of the future—you grew up, you got married, you lived happily ever after—but no concept of human growth, no clue how to accommodate the idea of growth into the marriage. Many marriages therefore crumbled when one or the other partner changed. And the idea of change and growth as a possibility for an older person was simply inconceivable. We all thought that we would sink into age and suddenly stop growing, like a dead plant. Of course it's all ridiculous, but that's the destiny we expected. What a revelation to find out that the human issues remain the same, that as long as we're alive, we're changing and growing minute by minute, and that that's not a bad thing, it's a good thing! Sometimes it takes a lifetime to learn the most obvious things.

Of course life does impose limits as we age, particularly limits of the body, as opposed to the mind. I no longer say, "if I die," but "*when* I die." I understand that my body has certain limitations, such as flexibility and upper-body strength, although even these can be extended by proper nutrition and exercise. It's kind of sad to realize that there are some things I will never do: compose an opera or write a great novel. But in the struggle to overcome limits, there's another refinement in one's thinking. You learn that some limits are real and some are self-imposed, or extracted from the culture in a way that doesn't have to be a self-fulfilling prophecy. In youth, if somebody said, "No, you can't do that," I would accept it. Now, I no longer accept "No, you can't." It may turn out that in fact I can't, but now I'm the one who learns through trying it whether or not I can. Often I fail, but there's something worthwhile in the attempt, I believe.

Last summer, I participated in a week-long women's religious retreat in which one of the courses offered was called "Embodying the Spirit." It helped me confront one of my weaknesses, my aversion toward my body ever since my mastectomy. When I told the instructor that I wouldn't take part in the *mikvah*, the ritual bath ceremony, she said, "Go, you'll give a gift." I replied that I hadn't come there to give a gift, that I didn't think I was ready to give this gift. I struggled all week with the question of whether I was protecting myself from the scrutiny of other people or protecting *them* from the ugliness of my single-breasted body. I had been conducting an informal group for women over forty-five, in which we were discussing our reactions to the ageism of American culture. The night before the scheduled bath ceremony, one woman began to disclose her own discomfort about her appearance ever since menopause. It turned out that so many of the older women had their own fears and worries about public exposure—feeling that their bodies were all wrong, too fat, too saggy, too old, too this, too that. I decided—pushing another limit—that maybe I would try it. So twelve of us—all terribly self-conscious—took part in the ceremony. It turned out that we were all so concerned about helping each other that we forgot about how we looked. Then we looked around at each other and started to laugh; it was really funny how we came in all shapes and sizes, all ages, all in varying degrees of imperfection. That laughter was cleansing. It helped us all to heal a bit in this area of accepting our own bodies, realizing we were all created in God's image.

Many women approached me later to thank me for giving them this gift, and all the while I was thinking how much the giving benefited *me*.

We go through every difficult experience once. By the time we get to it the second time, we know what to expect. As an infant, we play peekaboo with our mothers, learning that when Mommy disappears, she will soon come back. So at certain times, when unsummoned memories come around to haunt me, I know, having been there once, that there will be no surprises, that there's nothing either bad or good that I haven't experienced at least once. Eventually the bad moment will end, I will go on, I will leave for Japan soon, whatever bad thing I'm going through is not going to kill me. Although it's the kind of knowledge that comes with age, it starts when life starts, accumulating what you will eventually know.

My karate master, Kaisho Tadashi Nakamura, teaches that before every class, we must empty our minds before we can learn anything. Although every candidate for a black belt is already an advanced brown belt, one takes the test for the black belt wearing a white belt, to symbolize this idea of an empty mind, in which there are no preconceptions, only an openness and a readiness. That's how I think we should go about this business of living, so that toward the end, no matter what happens after we die, at least we can believe that we have learned something.

TINY DEATHS,
REBIRTHS

✑ *Zoë Caldwell, 62* ✑

Zoë Caldwell began acting professionally at the age of nine in her native Australia. In 1958, she earned a coveted scholarship to Stratford-on-Avon in England, then joined Canada's Stratford Festival Theater, where she first gained fame as a Shakespearean actress. Now an internationally renowned classical actress and theater director, she received two Tony Awards for her portrayal of Polly in Tennessee Williams's Slapstick Tragedy *and as Miss Brodie in* The Prime of Miss Jean Brodie *on Broadway. She currently holds the Eminent Scholar Chair at Florida State University, where she teaches acting. She is married to the Broadway producer Robert Whitehead; they have two sons, Sam and Charlie.*

On Turning Fifty

I'm a woman decidedly blessed
But about to turn fifty and oh yes, you guessed
I'm beginning to ask myself what have I done
with this half century under the sun?

I've had offers, won prizes, been lauded and panned,
I've taken some risks but I've never been banned
From a theater or union or city or land
and now I'm turning fifty.

I married a man who is almost a prince
And we've lived ever afterwards happily since
With two glorious sons. So then why do I wince?
It's because I'm turning fifty.

Now thank God I'm normal, whatever that means,
And have no desire to be back in my teens
And I really feel that I'm quite full of beans
For a woman who's turning fifty.

So how do I cope? Do I lie down and die?
Or sit in the corner and have a good cry?
Or drink lots of bourbon and get myself high
Because I'm turning fifty?

Hellpecker no! I know what I'll do . . .
I'll play *Medea* in Australia and direct *The Shrew*

and I'll try to live well 'til a hundred and two
And thank God that I'm turning fifty!

—Zoë Caldwell

I remember when my fiftieth birthday was approaching, I had a horrible time reconciling myself to it. Of course it's pure hubris, but I remember so clearly thinking, "I'm halfway through my life!" Which is ridiculous! Who lives to a hundred? And none of the other zeros in any way had any impression upon me at all. Except coming up to fifty, I got into a big-time depression, moaning and weeping and unable to sleep at all. I roamed the house at night, worrying. And I was always apologizing for myself: "Oh, I'm terribly sorry, is it too hot? Oh, I'm sorry, it's just too cold. Oh, I'm terribly, terribly, terribly sorry, forgive me but . . ." Always apologizing and asking forgiveness. I didn't understand it, of course, and was convinced I was going mad. And it was the same time as my menopause, so the two went hand in hand, the awareness of the withdrawal of the potential of life and this terrible, terrible conviction that I was going mad.

So I thought, Well, if I'm going mad, I'd better make a plan for when I'm not here—because clearly I'll be . . . not here. I'll be dead or something. Or institutionalized. So I'll keep it secret—the fear, I mean, of going mad that happens during the menopause. I succeeded in keeping my secret for four months or so, but eventually I blurted out to Robert that I was going mad. And he said, "Have you called Dr. Parks?" And I said, "No, no, no, it has nothing to do with gynecology, don't you understand I'm going mad?" And he said, "Well, I'd ring Dr. Parks anyway if I were you." And I did. Dr. Parks said, "Oh, you're going through menopause, I'll give you some tablets," and ten days later it was all gone. Completely gone! The depression, the sadness, the loss of confidence—gone. And then once I rounded the corner to fifty, I was absolutely fine!

I always tell women, when they feel they're going mad, Don't hide it, don't keep it a secret. Tell someone, tell your husband or your best friend, then tell your doctor you want hormones. You'll feel absolutely yourself again ten minutes later.

I feel these days a continual opening up and peeling away of defenses. I call it "tiny deaths, rebirths." Everybody's talking about lifting their faces and peeling their faces and I think, No! Peel away your *armor*. Peel away your walls and your shells and your defenses and get out there and *live*! And so what if you're crumpling here and crumbling there and your face is all wobbly and floppy and creased because of long life, don't bother lifting and peeling, because it's all just going to fall down again, anyway!

It's true, of course, that I'm dying, I mean bits and pieces of me are dying all the time, and the whole direction of gravity is not so swell. It's all *downward*, toward the grave. But so what? Life feels richer and fuller at this age for that very reason—the closeness to mortality and all that.

I was born and brought up an Episcopalian, but I never had much formal religion, or felt I needed it. Yet in recent years, my spirituality has deepened—my belief in the continuance of life, that whatever is contributed by each and every human being who's ever lived on earth will not be wasted—all of that has become stronger lately. That the resonance goes on and on and on and on, to life everlasting.

It's terrific, the freedom one can feel at this age. For instance, I have more confidence with who and what I am. I feel sexier than ever. I go dancing and dance my ass off, all night long. I'm always so pleased and amazed that my body still works! I'm not miserable with the way I look—I'm not thrilled, but I'm not miserable, I can handle it. I know I can't do everything I used to do, but what the hell, I can still do a lot. Most important, for the first time in my life, I really feel, deep down, that I'm okay. Not grand and great and grandiose, but just okay. And being okay is a lot.

The secret, I think, is to forget about oneself. We're all so *I*-centered. The advertising industry contributes greatly to that. "Buy the right kind of toothpaste and you'll be better. For *me*! For *my* mouth and *my* hair with the right shampoo and *me* and *me* and *mine*! *My* car, *my* vacation, *my* clothes, for *me* and *me* and *I*!" We have to get away from ourselves, and a good way to do that is to do any kind of work. It absolutely doesn't matter if you're working in McDonald's or selling shoes, work at something, anything. Love is also good, to help you get away from yourself. It doesn't have to be romantic love—just caring for someone and taking care of someone. Or just to be so goddamn busy cooking and cleaning and running around that you can leave yourself behind for those moments. The opposite of self is others. And that's the whole point of being alive, I believe. Forgetting self.

I don't think old has anything to do with being sixty. The disaster of "old" is when you don't have a sense of humor, are too focused on "I," and impatient with yourself and with others. I've always been hyper-hypercritical (being a Virgo), so I had to learn to stop judging myself so harshly. I had to learn tolerance, particularly for the "bad Zoë" I often was, to integrate with the "good Zoë." It took a long time for me to learn to accept myself, being so critical, to accept the bad parts along with the good parts. Forgiveness and acceptance and tolerance, all those boring old virtues, but one has to learn them. And humility, oh yes, let us never forget humility. I spend a lot of my time teaching now, and I always tell my students who are trying to learn acting, "Always remember, we are not, as actors, the godhead; we are the priests and priestesses taking the word of the playwright out of the temple to the populace. We're merely the conduit, like a plumber's pipe." Well, that's certainly a lesson in humility for the kids, a necessary lesson for all actors, for all human beings to learn. But life wants us to learn these things, the lessons are all around us. And that is the great task. All we have to do is look around.

MY NAKED EYES

ஐ Grace Slick, 54 ஒ

Grace Slick was the lead singer and songwriter for the Jefferson Airplane, a rock and roll group whose concerts became famous throughout the world as "Be-Ins" and "Happenings" that personified the acid days of the sixties. In the late seventies, after the group separated, Grace Slick and Paul Kantner— the father of her daughter, China, now an aspiring actress—formed the Jefferson Starship, which broke up for the last time in 1989. Except for a benefit concert in January 1995, she hasn't performed publicly in six years. Her house in Mill Valley, California, burned down last year and she recently moved to Los Angeles.

Your love talks inside me, words that no one hears.
Your love walks inside me, fear just disappears.
How I used to fool myself, confusing dark with light
Looking through my shadow life for suns that burn at
    night. . . .

—from a song in progress by Grace Slick

Last night I saw a movie, *A Streetcar Named Desire*. There were a considerable number of people laughing, the same way at the same time, as though they were all watching a sitcom together. I wondered why they were all laughing at something that is so transparently not a comedy but a tragedy. Was it because of all that sitcom training we're getting, that we're conditioned to laugh in the designated places while watching a woman having a nervous breakdown in a living room? Or was it because it was too painful to look at life the way it really is, to identify with Blanche as a woman who could be them, could be you, me, could be all of us? She doesn't have a chance and she knows it and is living in a fantasy land, and people keep nipping at that and ripping it apart, and pretty soon she just dissolves.

The way Blanche was treated by the other characters in the movie is a tiny paradigm of how older women are treated in society. Blanche's tragedy was that she saw herself as others saw her—as a pathetic, desperate, aging, time-to-retire flirt whose only hope was to find a man. It can make you as nuts as Blanche if you just sit around and feel sorry for yourself, grasping at straws, unable to face the truth. Sure, it hurts, but there it is, and facing the truth is itself a liberating venture.

When I get really old, I hope I can be like Ruth Gordon's character in *Harold and Maude*—doing whatever I please, appreciating the moment and being as wacko as I want.

I'm sorry to admit that the aging process, physically, is still frightening to me. Knowing that the male of the species is drawn to visual stimuli, the prospect of everything sagging and the chins and upper arms flapping in the breeze is still very scary. I go through periods of being highly interested in sex, and then I can go for months not even thinking about it. I only hope that when I get really old, and nobody is even looking at me as a possible "sperm object," I'll be in one of my celibacy phases and not even miss it.

There's so much artifice associated with being a woman. I don't only mean the mascara, the makeup, but worrying about whether "he" or "they" will like what I'm saying, will accept this or that, will find me attractive or not. So, without even realizing it, you censor yourself in order to be well-liked, or loved. For years, until I was about *fifty*, I would never leave the house without my eye makeup on. Now I no longer try to look like anything I'm not; I figure if some guy, even one I'm sexually attracted to, doesn't accept me as I am, so be it. I won't be getting up at five o'clock in the morning to put on my eye makeup so my lover won't see my naked eyes.

My parents' ironic nickname for me as a kid was "Grouser," like calling a rabbit "Killer." Nothing particularly bothered me. My father, an investment banker, was shy and reserved; my mother, who had been a singer before her marriage, was outgoing with a kind of quiet wit, but neither of them were big talkers. Since it was a quiet house, I had my eyes and ears open. I looked around and noticed how people conducted themselves, formed my own opinions about everything, and spent a lot of time by myself, drawing, painting, writing stupid little poems, dressing up—all indoor stuff. I'm not built for athletics.

I had always hoped and assumed I would grow up looking

like my mother, who was an absolutely *gorgeous* natural platinum blond, but that never happened. Once as a child I saw a Betty Grable movie and I immediately figured out that blond and cute were the things to be. But at puberty I went from pudgy and blond to stick-thin and black hair in an era where the ideal of femininity was to look like a Barbie doll. It annoyed me no end, the way I was constructed physically. I inherited my mother's pale eyelashes and eyebrows and my father's fuzzy hair. I would have liked longer legs and better hair, instead of the SOS pad I had then and still have, and was completely disgusted by my fat knees. Appearance, being attractive, being accepted—I took all that very seriously, as I think most teenagers do. Even grunge rockers have to have exactly the right beat-up flannel shirts.

It took me almost my whole life before I was able to come to terms with my appearance. At thirteen, I realized that I was never going to be Betty Grable. Years later, when I got a job as a model at I. Magnin, I figured, Well, if they want to hire me, I can't be *too* bad to look at. Then when I started singing, it got a little easier, to look like me. I still look at my knees in the mirror and think, "I'm going to have to cover those fuckers up." But now I realize that if I had been Betty Grable, my life would have turned out very differently. Because if you're not Betty Grable, you have to find out what else you've got that you can use or enjoy that overrides your ability to just hang around and be lovely.

The fifties were such a drab decade. To me, it looked like a *petit mort*, especially for women. What were you doing in the fifties if you were a woman? Well, clearly, you were in the house, cooking a bunch of food, picking up the snot on the carpet, going to the grocery store to buy more food, going to the bridge club, coming home to make dinner, which the kids and the husband expected to be on the table on time. You might have been planning with your hubby whether or not to buy another car, or hoping to scrape together enough to buy your way into a country club. This was what life was like day after day after day. That did not look like much fun to me. I was never really trained or pushed into housewifeness, I think because my mother thought, "Well, this kid is not a domestic, nurturing, caretaking type and she'll probably do something in the arts." Once I asked her, "Do you like cooking?" and she said, "Not particularly, it's just something that has to be done, like brushing your teeth." That's how I feel about it. My parents always more or less assumed, without really pushing about it, that I was going to work and support myself, maybe in the arts or in advertising. We all knew I wasn't going to be working for Lockheed or McDonnell Douglas as an electrical engineer. My mother had decided that she wouldn't do to me what *her* mother did to her, which was to constantly nag her to achieve in school. My grades in high school were just average; I did what I had to to maintain a B-minus average and spent the rest of the time socializing. I was simultaneously intimidated by and attracted to the most popular kids, one of them a girl named Darlene—a blonde, cheerleader, funny, adventurous—who is still a friend of mine. That was obviously where the deal was. Intellectuals didn't interest me unless they were also good-looking.

I spent my freshman year at Finch College in New York, where wealthy girls who didn't get good enough grades to get into Vassar were taught how to pour tea and get a Princeton husband so they would never again have to worry about getting good grades. I went because I wanted to go to New York and hang out. During Easter vacation some friends and I went to the Bahamas, which I loved so much I wanted to move there, but since there wasn't a college on Nassau, I went the following year to the University of Miami in Florida, which then had the reputation of being fun, lots of yucks. And it *was* fun, but after that I had had enough of college.

When I came back to San Francisco from Miami, I felt the first intimations of the sixties. One of my friends, Bill Piersoll, wanted to be a writer; Darlene was busy being a nouveau Communist, talking about "power to the people," and the winds of change were in the air. I was writing, too—mediocre poetry that could be put to music if you tortured it badly enough, and then translated into three-, four-, or five-chord songs. I was never busy *being a poet*, just trying to rhyme thoughts and stick them into a simple song. What I liked best about the sixties was that you could *wear* any goddamn thing you wanted to— as a kid I loved to dress up, so I appreciated that very much— and *look* any way you wanted to, and *say* anything you wanted to. Before the sixties came along, I felt restricted—so many parameters, so many rules and regulations. The sixties were like loosening a corset.

My first job after quitting college was as a receptionist for a group of lawyers. I was fired after two days because I'm not good at kissing ass. Then I started working as a floor model for the couturier department at I. Magnin. That year I heard the Jefferson Airplane singing at a small club in San Francisco, and I thought, "That looks *very* cool because they get paid more than I do, they only have to work a couple of hours a night, and they get free drinks." So some friends and I formed a group and we began playing the clubs, sometimes opening up for the Airplane or the Grateful Dead. Then Jefferson Airplane's lead singer decided to get married and move to Seattle. Since I was a tall brunette like her and had the same low voice, they asked me to join. The group had already made a record. About a year later, the skyrocket happened: The media decided to go find out about all these weirdos dressing funny, making music, so we got free publicity, the record companies thought they could make some money from it, and we made *Surrealistic Pillow*, which was a huge and unexpected success.

The success lasted for more years than we had anticipated.

We were all young, white, well-paid, living in California, getting recognized in rock and roll. Everything was just fine. We took acid and watched the walls melting and listened to marvelous music and thought, Wow, isn't this other-worldly, and believed that the world was changing and that we were on the cusp of an incredible social revolution—that there would be less conflict, fewer wars, and more love. Then in the early seventies I began to realize that this was not going to happen, or at least not very soon. That was a depressing thought. The mistake we made was that we had a naive belief in education; we thought that if we could just sit down with people and talk to them, or get them to read, we could instantly change their minds, get them to see the light. What we didn't yet understand was that the planet with all its species goes through evolution, and evolution takes time.

In the late seventies, I stopped singing and performing for a while. I should have stopped five years earlier, but dragged it on too long—ignoring the fact that the revolution wasn't happening, trying not to see that, to acknowledge that I was hurt by that. The seventies are often described, snidely, as the era of Studio 54, where everyone was taking a lot of Quaaludes and wearing Halston clothes and seeing how stupid they could get. The music turned into a synthesizer beat with lyrics like "Come on dance with me, babe." Nobody was saying anything of importance. The movie *Saturday Night Fever* came out, with its theme of "Can I win the dance contest?" That is not my scene. Airplane broke up and Starship was formed. It was a commercial era—our songs were not written by the group but by professional songwriters—and Starship had more hits than Airplane. But I was feeling as though half of me was imitating myself and the other half was just putting in time, like going to a job that has grown stale.

In 1989, I developed a shoulder injury called bilateral capsulitis, which means "frozen shoulder." I couldn't raise my left arm, reach up to do my makeup or my hair, or lift a microphone. Clearly, my body was telling me not to do this thing anymore, but I was too stubborn to admit it. That symptom was telling me about my alienation, which translated into giving the world the *cold shoulder*. If you don't work out your conflicts, your body will work them out for you, I believe. So when my body closed down, shut off, and said, "Stop!," I realized that I had to quit. I canceled that last concert and, except for one benefit concert, haven't performed since.

There's a Chinese curse that says, "May you live in interesting times." Anything *interesting* is going to be volatile, and anything volatile is going to have, inevitably, the extremes of good and bad. That can be a potent mixture: It means that we're going to have to grow whether we want to or not. Even the fifties were interesting, because they were the womb of the sixties; if we didn't have that repression, we wouldn't have needed to leap out the way we did.

We've all lived through interesting times, experienced both ends of that burning candle—Kent State, Vietnam, the peace movement, finding out that our presidents were lying to us, the civil rights movement, the disco seventies, the rise of feminism, the reaction against all of that, the Yuppie eighties, and now, possibly the most interesting and transformative era of all, the one we're in now: As Ram Dass said, "If you thought the sixties were interesting, wait till you see the nineties." This decade is still young, and right now it looks like everything is falling apart—marriages, families, the environment, school systems, institutions. Our song lyrics show the hopelessness, the despair of young kids. Usually songs are about love or "Let's go boogie" or "Down with the president"; now they're about teenage suicide. But sometimes there is so much chaos that we forget that something new, possibly better, is brewing. Out of the mud grows the lotus. What we're seeing now is the last gasp of "Gimme everything," which was what we saw in the eighties, and the destruction that comes before a new and more spiritual condition—something of beauty and value that will grow out of the chaos we see all around us. We're moving out of "me me me" and into "us us us!"

There are certain stages you have to go through in order to learn. You can't jump from the bottom rung of the ladder to the top; you've got to live the stuff in between—a succession of life's events, a unique ladder of information. Every person has unique experiences, some of them difficult, devastating. At the bottom of the ladder, we're young and invincible. The middle of the ladder is change, loss, betrayals, disillusionment, deaths. The top of the ladder is wisdom, or enlightenment—a rare spiritual condition. For me, the process has felt like a chipping away of what I don't really need anymore, like a sculptor pares away the clay to get at the shape within. My soul feels lean like a runner; a lot of *junk* is getting pared away—neuroses, habits, confusions. Thirty years ago, I felt that I needed to make a good impression, physically, intellectually, and professionally. I wanted to be *cool*. Now, even if it's not cool, I'll say, "No, I haven't read that, I don't know what you're talking about," or admit that I don't know how to use a computer. I won't try to pretend anymore, about anything. Maybe it's because, as I've gotten older, it just seems like too much effort to lie—you have to remember the lie. Or maybe it's just that the truth has become more important to me now.

The last big wall to come down is my ability to show vulnerability. I used to have two basic masks in my repertoire: Either everything is fine, or I'm angry. But it was never "Help me, I'm hurting," never showing anguish, never crying. The last thing I would say to someone who was leaving me is "Don't leave me." I'd say, "Be my guest." Where I once tended to keep people at a distance, I'm now able to tell them how much I appreciate them, how much in need of their company I am. I can say, "Damn, you just blow me away!" rather than worrying about whether that's going to make me look like a doormat. I'm still not all the way there yet. Even now, I still fight impulses to cry. Driving home from the movie last night, I found myself fighting the desire to cry out loud over the fate of Blanche DuBois. I've been so used to keeping those masks on that I've been able, until very recently, to fool even myself. Maybe I'm afraid I'll dissolve forever into tears once I let them go.

It's only very recently that I've begun to agree with that old cliché "You get what you give." I always thought that giving everything away might mean I'd be left with nothing. Now I know that there's an endless supply of stuff in there to give, and that it doesn't diminish me in any way to keep on giving.

For the last few years, I've been leading a very quiet, placid life. I don't mean that I've entered a nunnery, or that I sit around contemplating my navel, but I have more time to sort things out now. That kind of time—solitary, quiet, thoughtful—is good for the spirit. About four or five years ago, I began reading about and working with animal rights organizations. That started when I began putting out food for the raccoons every night. People talk about becoming a born-again Christian or seeing the white light, but having a wild animal come up to me, look me right in the eye and *hold my hand*—actually caressing the interior of my palm to find out who I am—well, that was one of the most amazing things that ever happened to me. I'd spend hours watching the raccoons; they'd come up to the house and tap on the window and I'd lean out the window and hand them a cookie. Each time they played with my fingers, I'd think, "I'm falling in love with a raccoon!" I'd go to my friend's pet store, read about biomedical research, and eventually got more and more involved in trying to help animals, and all of that took me out of myself and into the knowledge that *we* are not the most important things on earth. Experiences like that, I believe, make us a little less self-absorbed. A little more willing to, or actively desirous of, doing those things that make *us* (as opposed to *me*) happy. It's still actually kind of selfish, because working in the service of *us* makes you happy, but it's a better kind of selfishness. Even Mother Teresa is in it for a payoff—she wants to live a life where she feels she has done something to help. I hate to use the word *grace*, because that's my name, but it has that quality—of being blessed, of being offered a gift. You can only find that out when you start working for something besides yourself. And it all comes back a thousand times over.

My parents died within a couple of years of each other. One night, about a month after my mother died, I was lying in bed reading and I heard her voice saying "Grace?" That was it, just that one word. And I was thinking, "Oh, man, here comes one of these deals where you're hearing a disembodied voice talking to you." Not even on acid did I ever experience anything that far out. I said, "Yeah, Mom, are you calling me?" I waited for a few moments, but nothing happened; she didn't say anything else. But that experience added another little piece to the puzzle, or stripped a little piece away from my defensive insistence on believing only what I can see and touch. Another layer was pared away—mistrust, nonacceptance, skepticism. The fact that people you love just go away and are not there anymore is another one of those hard truths, but it's all part of the ladder, another rung on the way up to understanding. Life deals out these things, to everybody, and you can either get enraged about it or figure out some way to express your anguish, so you don't have to go out and murder someone. So it would behoove us all to find some sort of radical behavior that could provide a creative outlet for that rage, that pain. It could be sewing, it could be throwing pots, keeping a journal, making afghans— anything at all! I happen to do it in mediocre poetry. Many women implode and get depressed, instead of expressing their anger. But I think it's healthier to get it all out there, to vent it, express it, any way you can. I only just realized that, like yesterday. Which proves, perhaps, that we're never too old to grow. As Gandhi said: "My commitment is to the truth, not to consistency."

GIVE IT UP

⤳ Joan Ganz Cooney, 65 ⤳

Sesame Street, *the award-winning television program for preschool children,
was originated by Joan Cooney in 1968. She was a cofounder, president,
and CEO of the Children's Television Workshop, which also created* The
Electric Company, 3-2-1 Contact, Square One TV, *and* Ghostwriter.
*Children's Television Workshop programs have been awarded sixty-six
Emmys and have been seen by millions of children throughout the world.
Now chairman, since 1990, of the executive committee of the Children's
Television Workshop board, she has been married for fifteen years to her
second husband, former Secretary of Commerce Peter Peterson, a New York
investment banker.*

After her husband died, Eleanor Roosevelt became the first role model I had. Before that, she was someone people made fun of. I had never seen a woman make it on her own, instead of riding on her husband's coattails, in such a public way, and I was deeply impressed with her. Primarily, though, like many women who chose to build a career, I identified with men. Most successful women are androgynous, I believe, with a kind of permanent man/woman tension in them. This can be a great source of conflict for women with families. On the one hand, we identified with our fathers as much, or more, than our mothers. On the other hand, that whole conventional upbringing is also in us, so that we try to make ourselves available to husband, children, while constantly trying to maintain these high professional standards. It can really wear you out when your conventional self is constantly warring against your unconventional self, the self that is successful in business. That fear of criticism, which I got from my mother, who was a real critic, keeps you forever trying to stay ahead of that little critical voice that says, "Have you been to see that grandchild? Are you ready for Easter?"

I've worked a great deal on this perfectionism of mine, and I'm finally to the point where I can say, "Give it up, Joan. Who do you think you are that you're supposed to be meeting all these demands . . .?" It's been repeatedly pointed out to me that no one, except my family, would miss a beat if I gave up some control, or in fact if I just suddenly disappeared completely. Once you have created something, that creation takes on a life of its own, and one must allow it to do so, just as parents must, eventually, let their children grow up and away.

I was very driven when I was a young woman—very nervous, very high-strung, always going flat-out, always running scared—scared of failure, I suppose, scared of my own shadow. I was the third of three kids, and constantly drove myself to keep up with my older siblings. It wasn't so much that my parents put that idea into my head, but I seem to have been born with a terribly high standard of perfection, and a constant anxiety that I wouldn't measure up. Every time I got a grade below an A, I felt like a total failure. In childhood, I suffered greatly from loneliness and social isolation. I was always trying to be with the older kids, and when I couldn't measure up, I would go home and read, and that became my world.

But in high school, unlike most teenagers, I had the time of my life. I took up acting and was recognized and accepted for my budding talent. I was popular for the first time, which pleased my hypercritical mother. Being popular, doing well in school, getting some small recognition for acting made me feel that I had at last done something that seemed to meet my mother's aspirations for me. My upbringing was very conventional, very traditional, meaning that girls should be womanly, and boys, manly. On the other hand, there was another, conflicting message that got through to me. Although I think my mother would have been perfectly happy if I had married a rich guy young, I also got the message that she didn't want me to be a traditional wife like herself. She sort of protected me from domestic things like washing the dishes and cleaning the house, and in fact, whenever it was time for me to participate in these domestic duties, I always got a stomachache. But I did get the feeling that she wanted me to aspire to something beyond marriage and children, toward some sort of public achievement.

That must have been what prevented me from marrying too soon. In those days, you could not easily have a career along with a husband and children, not if you grew up in the forties. I was already thirty-four when I got married. We had no children, not by choice, and I think that is partially what drove me to become involved with children. After college, I worked as a newspaper reporter, which qualified me to become a press agent for television shows, the *U.S. Steel Hour* and various shows at NBC. It was very unchallenging work, and I couldn't see how I could get from that to something more interesting. Then I read that the Educational Broadcasting Corporation had acquired Channel 13, and I moved heaven and earth to get a job there and did, in 1962, as a producer. That was the day I was born.

My husband and I were very much part of the sixties and the civil rights movement and so on. He was a radical feminist—in those days, anyone who talked about equality between men and women was considered radical—and in fact, I certainly thought it was a radical idea myself. Equality? I had never heard of such an outlandish idea, couldn't get my mind around it. Like almost every other woman of my generation, I thought that women were born to be wives and mothers first, and number two, or even further down than that, in the workplace. I thought that we were the more fragile, less aggressive sex and that you couldn't really succeed without that aggressiveness. I can't believe how stupid I was.

Yes, it is true that women are less aggressive than men, but now I believe that this comparative absence is a big strength in the workplace. You don't need sharp elbows to succeed—what you need are political and psychological skills, interpersonal skills, which women have developed to a high degree. Aggressiveness suggests hostility, whereas assertiveness, which is a gentler quality, has no hostility in it. In an organization like this, you do not see aggression on either side, men or women. *Sesame Street* is a culture of cooperation. Is there competition? Yes. Backbiting? Sure. But compared to most organizations, there is probably less testosterone here than most others.

There are still certain businesses—investment banking, for

example—in which women do have a hard time, perhaps because they don't aspire to the twelve-, fourteen-, sixteen-hour days, the very sharp elbows. If they start working in these fields, at some point they usually stop, saying, "What's it all about? This is not for me." Women are different, and that is a big plus. An excess of testosterone is an advantage in some organizations, but in most, estrogen is a far bigger advantage.

I think "youth" is highly overrated. I know I certainly didn't have much fun in my twenties and thirties, and never even felt appreciated as a woman until I met my second husband, at forty-nine. My first marriage was difficult and demanding. My husband was an alcoholic, and even though he was highly supportive of my career, there was very little going on in my life except taking care of him and burying myself in work. I did a lot of traveling, and resented it very much when I would be eating alone and some man would ask if he could join me. So I always ordered meals from room service. Actually, I found that I was really kind of relieved to have that physical attractiveness, that nubileness, behind me. I find it liberating, now, to walk into a room somewhere and not have anyone eyeing me. And when I went through menopause, I blessed every one of my hot flashes, which were like candles on a birthday cake. I suffered terribly from PMS, where for a week I'd be teary and depressed. So the joy of having that over with was marvelous. I would sit at parties and would feel this intense heat, then this little sea breeze, and I would say, "At last!"

Sesame Street went on the air when I was just shy of forty—not so late in life that I was embittered, nor so early that it disoriented me—and a few years later my marriage ended, which deeply saddened me. It was the death of something, a loss, even though it was of my own choosing. A friend who had been through a divorce and a remarriage called me and said, "If I were younger, I'd say I'm sorry." He knew, in a way that I didn't, at the time, that it wasn't a tragedy, but it took me a long time to get over that sadness, that guilt. I did what I usually did, buried myself in work. It took an enormous effort to build an endowment that would stabilize the company and allow it to become fully independent. We started in 1968 with grants from foundations and from the government, but it wasn't until about fifteen years later that we finally achieved complete financial independence, when I could feel that the company would outlast me.

I remarried at the age of fifty, to a man with enormous gifts, unlimited energy. He has five children, the youngest of whom was then nine, one of whom is retarded. Suddenly my personal life became even more complicated with, eventually, new and unanticipated rewards. The rule of stepmotherhood is that you must stay the course, give the time, take the trouble, pay attention to the feelings of ambivalence, at best, of your stepchildren. Divorce alone is so difficult for children, and they were entirely alienated, emotionally, from the idea of their parents divorcing after twenty-five years, and their father remarrying so soon. But I stuck with it and now couldn't be any closer to my stepchildren. My relationship with them has been one of the most enriching things in my life, watching them get married and becoming a grandmother.

Recently my husband was negotiating to hire someone for his company, and oh, the *Sturm und Drang* around this hire was just so extraordinary. At one point he said, "I think it's going to flake away," and I said, "Let it. When somebody is so uncertain about being with you, they shouldn't be with you." And I thought, that's something you learn. Let it go. Sometimes what you think you want isn't the best thing. I bless every job I was turned down for, every house that got sold while I was looking at it, because something else always turned up instead, and it usually turned out much better than what I originally wanted so desperately. I remember when I was in my thirties and working at Channel 13, *desperately* trying to get work in network news, but no one would hire me. Now I bless all those guys who turned me down. I'm so grateful for some of the things that *didn't* happen, as well as the sad things that *did* happen, because everything led to something else.

I was brought up Catholic—very lapsed now. Most people don't have a clue what it really means to be a Christian. It was always supposed to be about helping people, taking care of the poor, "the least of these my brethren," but no one wants to do that. There's a gospel spiritual that says, "My God is real because I can feel him in my soul." That sums up my personal religion. Is there an afterlife? I don't know. But there is something that connects us all and humanizes us all. I sense it in certain music—jazz, spirituals, opera—and in poetry, feel that connection with others and that sense of joy. A shedding of all that getting and spending, all those meetings and appointments and commitments, all the houses and the *things* in them. I lead a much too busy and complicated life; I often get up in the morning and feel like a windup doll, running all the time, instead of living the true life of the spirit. I realize how foolish it is, that whatever this feeling is, that's what's real. *This* is what's important, *that* is not. So it's really a question of reorganizing my life to shed some of the commitments, so I won't feel guilty about not meeting them. That's what I've got to learn to do, to say *no*. There's only a limited quantity of fuel. So I have to say, "This is not going to fill the tank. How much gasoline is it going to use up?"

WHERE DOES IT GO?

✑ Judith Crist, 73 ✑

Judith Crist, one of the most accomplished movie critics in the United States, has been a journalist, editor, teacher, and movie and theater critic during a career that spans fifty-eight years. She has been teaching part-time at Columbia University's Graduate School of Journalism for more than thirty-five years. In 1987, she retired as a movie critic, but she continues to teach two classes a week at Columbia, where, she says, she still gets a vital shot of adrenaline from her students, and is at work on her first novel. Recently widowed, she is the mother of one son.

Nobody knew more than I thought I did when I was a young hotshot reporter. I was so full of myself, so sure that my words, my imperishable words, were right and absolutely nonnegotiable when editors tried to edit me. I fought like a tiger to keep everything I wrote exactly as I wrote it. But now I look back at my clips over the last forty or fifty years and realize how much I didn't know, how much room there was for improvement. I'm much more critical of my own writing now, and perhaps less critical of my students— not really less demanding, just slightly easier on them, more willing to give them a break—almost to the point of verbal constipation. Humility was a subject that didn't come up much in my younger years. Of course all writers need a tremendous ego just to want to become a writer in the first place, and to keep on believing in themselves no matter what.

Now that I'm older, I'm really much smarter, knowing how much I don't know. At the same time, I'm aware that I have managed to accumulate a certain amount of knowledge, and that knowledge is not only wanted but *needed* in today's information-overload world. There's a lovely new sense of being part of a continuum, of something larger than one's own petty concerns, of passing the torch, of generosity to all people, but particularly to the young. The person on the lower rung of the ladder should not be kicked aside, but should be offered a hand. We must pass on our hard-earned knowledge and experience to younger men and women. Older people make natural teachers.

I was a Depression baby, of the generation that went from the twelve-room house to the tiny apartment where the parents slept on the couch and the kids had the only bedroom. That particular generation, as compared with the postwar fifties kids, always seemed to understand that the only way out and up was through education and work. I always assumed that I would have a good job, and started very early—at the age of eight— applying for a job as a salesclerk at the corner candy shop. The manager looked at me as if I were crazy! "Are you kidding?" he howled. He gave me a lollipop and sent me home.

My mother was a librarian who gave up working to stay home with her children, but it was always understood that my future was going to be different. Books and learning were the way to that future. My mother and I were always reading together—separately, but together. On Saturdays, she would cook up a huge pot of cabbage—both my father and my brother hated cabbage, but my mother and I loved it—and the two of us would sit there eating cabbage leaves and reading, utterly absorbed, utterly happy. And whenever I got upset with my brother, or she got upset with her husband, my mother, who never learned how to drive a car, would joke, "You're going to learn how to drive a car, and as soon as you get your license, we're going to get in that car and leave these two men."

One of the differences between my generation and today's is that we knew how to keep our mouths shut. We didn't feel we had to tell the entire truth to everybody, to let it all hang out, as the jargon goes. In 1943, at the age of twenty-one, I had an abortion. The only person who knew about it was my best friend, a law student at Columbia, whose room I stayed in for a few days. I had five hundred dollars, so I was able to go to a fancy doctor up on Central Park West, and nobody, absolutely nobody else, knew. It would have been absurd to have a baby at that age and stage. And that fall, I went back to Pullman, Washington, where I had a teaching fellowship, and there was a woman doctor who told me, "I'm going to give you some equipment, and if you don't use it, you'll get in trouble again." She gave me a diaphragm. But I really would have died rather than discuss it with my mother. On the other hand, I always believed that my mother knew about a lot of things but had too much respect for me to probe into my private life.

That same year, instead of continuing my teaching fellowship in Pullman, I was hired by the Army Air Corps to teach English to prospective pilots, navigators, and bombardiers. It was an absolute smorgasbord of beautiful men! My mother came to visit for a week during that year, and I suspected that she knew my lifestyle, but she never said a word. I suppose she knew I wasn't going out robbing banks, so we colluded together, without ever talking about it, because she trusted me not to do anything too terrible and live my own life. We were a generation of great readers, and we learned about love and sex by reading the great novels. And of course we realized how silly it was to get married too young, before one is even formed yet, and marry merely because you wanted to make love. It was just plain silly, and most of the women I knew didn't fall into that trap.

The only reason my husband, Bill, and I decided to get married was that (a) he was sick and tired of eating in restaurants and (b) I was sick and tired of getting up at five in the morning and going home and pretending to be asleep in my own bed at seven o'clock in the morning when my father, by then widowed and living with me, woke up. I respected his feelings enough to obey the forms, but my private life was private.

My husband and I waited nine years before we had our son. We were of the divorce generation, and loved each other and wanted to stay married to each other, but we knew the only way to keep the marriage alive was for *both of us* to establish our careers before we had a child. And that, of course, was another blessing, because by the time Steven was born, I was mature enough to be a mother and absolutely delighted about it. And I had established myself as a journalist, so that the birth of my son didn't interrupt my working life too much.

The women I saw around me—let's call them prefeminism feminists—gave me the idea that I, as a woman, could do as I pleased. A woman I adored at Columbia University was Marjorie Hope Nicholson, one of the great eighteenth-century scholars of all time. She'd walk around the campus with her bun disintegrating and her slip showing and her stockings sagging around her ankles, and I thought she was just marvelous. I wanted to be exactly like her—someone too absorbed in things of the mind to give a damn how she looked. And I didn't see anything standing in the way of my having a wonderful career, if I wanted one. Which I did.

One of my neighbors, a man who retired a few years ago, asked me recently, "What do you *do* with all your time now?" He was simply at loose ends, not resourceful enough to figure out how many wonderful things there are in this world to do. Besides teaching two classes a week at Columbia, I love hanging out at odd hours at museums, and going to the movies in the afternoon, when all the senior citizens, who know how to keep their mouths shut at the movies, go. If I didn't have some self-respect, and if there wasn't Court TV, I would probably be one of those little old ladies in tennis shoes hanging around the federal courthouse or the Supreme Court watching the trials, predicting the outcomes, utterly obsessed with all those human stories, like those wonderful potboiler mystery novels. I love all that! And I've rediscovered reading, the way I used to as a kid, when I would borrow eight books from the library and read them far into the night, with a flashlight under the covers, devouring them with a hunger that I'm rediscovering now. And after a lifetime of being overregimented and having no time whatsoever for myself, I'm learning how to slow down, live at a more leisurely pace, and simply take the time to look at the river and the bird feeders and the squirrels.

I think we have great privileges when we reach a certain age. I like being obstreperous, speaking out all my prejudices in a way I never could before. I suppose I was always sort of opinionated and loudmouthed, but never with such *comfort*. I don't have to think of couching things I want to say to people in more bearable terms. I just come right out and say what's on my mind! I can dress exactly the way I please, and no longer have to feel a fool of fashion. Far more relaxed about appearance, I go for days without putting a drop of makeup on and don't give it a second thought. I suppose I could have my face lifted, but what for? It's a good old face, I've grown into it, I'm comfortable with it. It's a tragic spectacle to watch women, or men, for that matter, trying to hold on to youth too long.

I'm a fatalist. I don't particularly believe in an afterlife, but I do believe in a continuum. Sometimes I imagine that all the people I loved who have died are all together in some merry place, my father playing pinochle with his buddies, my mother reading books, my aunt Molly making her *fabulous* potato pudding, and Bill up there kibbitzing and maybe doing a little woodworking. The one thing I can't conceive of is that suddenly it will be blank. I'm too cynical to picture myself wandering around with a harp and a halo, but not cynical enough to conceive of coming to a halt.

My perception of time has changed most drastically. I don't know where the hell February went. And January. And wasn't it just last week that I was bitching about having to go to a film festival in Palm Beach in October? Wasn't it only yesterday, that family Christmas we all had up in the country? God, it all goes so fast. Where does it go?

When my neighbor, who was obviously dying of boredom, asked me what one does with all of one's time when retired, I thought, but didn't say, for a change, "Are you kidding?" Just look around, you'll find a million things you can accomplish, a million things you can contribute. No matter where you are, in a city or a small town or farming community, there's not a local hospital that doesn't need a volunteer, not a school in this country that doesn't need help teaching its children. A friend of mine, a magazine editor who was forced into retirement at sixty-five, began teaching a little Puerto Rican kid how to read two days a week. We can all share our experience and our maturity and our hearts and our souls and our minds with another generation. So I think we should force ourselves to get out of the house and *give* a little! And even if getting out means getting into the kitchen and trying to figure out a way to make pie crust, there's something to be done. Try what we haven't tried yet, investigate what we haven't learned yet, discover what we haven't discovered yet. We should all get up off our asses and stop concentrating on ourselves and what we haven't got, and the ways we've been mistreated, and get up, get out, and get at it.

FOOTPRINTS

∾ Mary Taylor Previte, 63 ∾

Mary Previte has been the administrator of the Camden County Youth Center, a pretrial facility for juveniles accused of serious crimes, for twenty years. Born in China of missionary parents, she spent three years in a Japanese concentration camp during World War II. Her autobiography, Hungry Ghosts, *recounts her own remarkable story: how a woman who learned hope as a prisoner of war teaches hope and "success skills" to teenaged prisoners of America's urban wars.*

I was fourteen years old when I lost my hand in a sawmill accident. My brother Johnny and I were staying with friends on a small island in rural Michigan while our parents were away. I had been out picking wild berries in the fields. I don't remember why I was standing next to the sawmill. I heard a loud *bump* and looked down to see that my hand had been split open by the saw. One minute, it was teenaged fingers nibbled at the fingernails and tanned skin stained with blueberry and strawberry juice, and the next minute a bloody mess. I awoke from surgery and immediately measured my bandaged arm against the other one, trying to guess whether or not I had a hand. That's when I saw that one arm was shorter than the other.

One morning a few months later, while my father was braiding my hair—I had not yet learned to braid with one hand—my brother came in and asked, "Can Mary still ride a bike?" My father replied, "I don't see why not." Those words, "I don't see why not," became a banner written across my sky. It is a motto that still speaks to me across the forty-nine years that have passed since that morning.

If you believe a child can do anything, he can. A parent's words can affect a child for life. A parent's words can jump-start the soul of a child. Conversely, a parent's words can wither the soul of a child in an instant. Hurtful words can have as lasting an effect as a physical beating. My mother insisted that I immediately switch from piano lessons to organ lessons, so that I could play with one hand and both feet. She taught me how to crochet with one hand. When I tried to play "puny, puny, oh no, I can't do it," she lined me up, strict and straight, and insisted that I help with the dishes like everyone else. Today, I sit and type stories for children with my one hand. I make quilts, which is my hobby, with my one hand; I wallpaper and paint my house with my one hand. I mow the lawn and work in the garden single-handedly, because forty-nine years ago, my father said, "I don't see why not."

I was born in a Bible school in Kaifeng, a compound deep in the interior of China. My father was a third-generation missionary who didn't believe in sitting in British enclaves and sipping tea. He felt that in order to reach the Chinese people, you had to go deep inside the borders, beyond the fringes, in places that had seen almost no white people before. "Foreign devils," the Chinese called anyone who was not born in China. But I never knew I wasn't Chinese. Our compound included American and British missionaries and Chinese students. We played with the Chinese, ate Chinese food, spoke Chinese; everything about the Chinese was what we liked and what we did. My *amah*, the lady who took care of me, was almost a mother to me. Her name was Er-dzieh, "Second Sister"—a little lady with tightly bound feet.

For centuries, the custom in China had been to bind the feet of five- or six-year-old girls—pushing the toes under, then binding them with excruciatingly tight muslin bandages. Since the toenails kept growing after the foot was bound, agonizing pain marked every step. My mother made it her personal crusade to stop this custom, which she saw as a way of controlling young women, of keeping them hobbled for life. The girls, who were usually betrothed in infancy, were told, "Your future husband wants his wife to have beautiful feet." Beautiful feet were tiny five-inch feet, shriveled, deformed feet, feet that would not allow a woman to stray too far from home and husband. But the custom died very slowly, even after it was outlawed by the Chiang Kai-shek government. Mothers hid their daughters under the bed or in large earthenware pots when the soldiers came to enforce the ban. So my mother's foot-unbinding crusade failed, because the Chinese women were just not ready to be liberated. Liberation comes first through the mind.

Every morning, the tradition in our house was to have a family worship service. My mother put the words from Psalm 91 to music: "He that dwelleth in the secret place of the most high shall abide under the shadow of the Almighty. A thousand shall fall at thy side and ten thousand at thy right hand, but death shall not come nigh thee. He shall give his angels charge over thee, to keep thee in all thy ways. . . ." And we would sing this psalm at our morning worship, and these promises from God were sung into our souls.

Japan, with an eye to geographical expansion, had been attempting to invade China for several years. They had already overrun the central province of Hunan, where my parents were working, and the order was that everyone had to bow to the Japanese captors. If my mother did not get off her bicycle fast enough to please the soldiers, she got hit with a stick. That's when my parents decided to take the two younger children to the boarding school at Chefoo, one of only a handful of English-speaking boarding schools in China that served the children of British and American businesspeople and missionaries, and where my older brother and sister, Jamie and Kathleen, were already enrolled. I was then seven years old.

China was already at war with Japan, but it was not "our" war, not the British or the West's war. The Japanese had gunboats in the harbor. We could hear the bullets flying overhead, into the mountains behind the city, and in the morning we would see the bloody bandages of the Chinese guerillas who had been struck by fire from the gunboats, the men limping as they passed along the road. When we heard the gunfire, my sister would grab us and pull us under the bed and say, "Dow kow li," which means, "Let's play." Our response to danger was to play and have fun. How could we be afraid? God had promised to keep us safe.

On December 8, 1941, the radio reported that the American fleet at Pearl Harbor was in flames. Two British battleships had been sunk off the coast of Malaya. We all woke up in the morning to find Japanese soldiers on our doorstep. They glued the seal of the Great Emperor of Japan on all the furniture, proclaiming that our beds, desks, blackboards, and all our school equipment no longer belonged to us but to the Emperor. A Shinto priest performed some kind of ceremony in the ball field, and suddenly, just like that, we were not free anymore. But our Latin master, Gordon Martin, did not let that mere fact deter his preparations for the school's Christmas puppet show. The Japanese sentries laughed at the puppets, which eased our fears. After that, we were never truly afraid of the Japanese again.

Meanwhile, my parents were working eight hundred miles away in the interior of China. When Pearl Harbor was struck, a Chinese student came rushing in to class to show my parents the headline: AMERICA AT WAR WITH JAPAN. My mother left the room and went into the bedroom, threw herself across the bed, and began to weep. She had read of the rape of Nanking, and all she could think about was her teenaged daughter, Kathleen. Would the soldiers rape Kathleen? And her son Jamie—would they conscript him into the army? And Johnny and Mary, the babies—what would happen to them? In her despair, she began to pray to God to protect her children. And she heard a voice in her mind saying, "If you look after the things that are dear to God, He will look after the things that are dear to you." Later she told us, "It was as though the tears had been wiped out of my heart. I understood that God and I had a pact. I was looking after the things that were dear to Him—the Chinese— and He was looking after the things that were dear to me."

A short time later, we were marched off to a concentration

camp—a snaking line of about two hundred children, carrying whatever we could in our hands, our teachers leading the way. The Chinese people along the route wept in disbelief as their friends and companions were marched past them, singing from the Psalms: "God is our refuge and strength, therefore we shall not fear." We were packed into three small houses, each one containing about eighty people, crammed in like sausages on the floor. Food was scarce and conditions were horribly over-crowded, but all the children made it into a game. We watched the Japanese conducting bayonet drills, heard them screaming "Yah!" as they lunged at each other with their fixed bayonets. We called it "Yah practice." Then, nine months later, the Japanese began a procedure of concentrating all these small enclaves of foreign prisoners into three immense concentration camps throughout China. The one we were taken to was called Weihsien.

If you ask a child what he needs to make him feel safe, he will say, "I want to know what's going to happen next." Our teachers created that structure. In the midst of every kind of human misery—near-starvation and dirt and heat and cold and plagues of bedbugs, rats, and flies—the Weihsien camp was run with superb discipline and organization. For some reason, the Japanese, who lived in separate houses adjacent to the camp, left the internal operation of the camp to the fourteen hundred prisoners installed there. There were people in charge of cook-ing, pumping water—my older brother, Jamie, was old enough for that job—scrubbing clothes, mending shoes, swabbing the slime pit of the latrine. When you woke in the morning, you heard a voice, always the same voice: "Up up up up up, time to get up!" Then you knew you had to scrub your teeth and wash your face in a basin. You knew when it was your turn at the latrine; you knew that every day you'd make your bed—a steamer trunk laid out with a thin cotton mattress—and scrub your little square piece of floor. Then you trooped off to breakfast, where you ate glop out of a soap dish or a tin can. Always the teachers insisted on discipline and good manners, saying, "You will sit up straight and you will talk softly. You will not talk with your mouth full. You will speak just as though you were one of the two princesses of Buckingham Palace. Because there is not one set of rules for the concentration camp and another for the *nice* world." You sat on the ground in the camp and wrote out your lesson on slates. You memorized Scriptures. You did these things every day, always at the same time of day, and that structure, that comforting predictability, just strengthened and sustained us during the whole three years we spent at Weihsien.

Years later, Miss Carr, the headmistress for younger children, told me she knew someday the prisoners would be forced to dig a trench and be lined up and machine-gunned to death; she prayed that when the time came, she would be one of the first to go. I was shocked to hear that she felt that way! The grown-ups knew that the Japanese army wasn't going to continue giving food to the prisoners, that they were going to keep it for themselves, but not the kids. Even the hardships—the shortages of food, the standing in the boiling heat of summer or the freezing snow of winter for daily roll call—were all a part of kids' play, kids' frolic, and kids' trust. We all felt safe, because of being protected by the teachers.

All through the war, there was never a doubt in our minds that we were going to win. Hadn't God promised that "A thousand shall fall at thy side, but death shall not come nigh thee?" We all knew someone would come to rescue us, but we couldn't know whether it was to be the Americans, the British, the Chinese, or the Russians. So every Tuesday night, behind the commandant's office, the Salvation Army Band practiced the national anthems of all the Allied powers, just to cover all the bases.

Though we had no contact with the outside world, rumors

were flying that the Japanese had surrendered. I remember that summer, the summer of 1945—the teachers had canceled school because of the heat. It was 120 degrees, so hot that we could hardly walk on the baked dirt of the compound. I was sick with dysentery and lying on my steamer trunk bed when I heard a buzzing noise. I looked out the window of the dormitory and saw a plane flying so low, it almost touched the treetops; I could see the American flag emblazoned on the belly of that plane. Then the belly opened and out poured these brilliant red, yellow, and white things that looked to me like giant flowers, like brilliant silk poppies, with tiny toy figures dangling from the end of them. Talk about instant cure for diarrhea! Standing in the fields outside the camp were seven American paratroopers. Fourteen hundred skinny, scraggly, emaciated prisoners poured out through the gates and into the field, hoisting these young American airmen up onto their bony shoulders and carrying them back to the camp. There on a mound near the gate, the Salvation Army Band was singing the American national anthem intermingled with "Happy Days Are Here Again." When the band got to the words "o'er the land of the free and the home of the brave," one trombone player, a young American student, fell to his knees and began to weep. The war was over.

Today, we are engaged in another war, equally bloody, equally pitiless—the war against children. Too many children in America live in terror. Terror freezes the brain. A sixteen-year-old boy says to me, "They'll bury me in Evergreen cemetery." A girl tells about ten or twelve of her friends who were killed by drive-by shootings this year. A boy says, "I hate my dad, he ain't never there." A twelve-year-old girl says, "Do you know how it feels to be raped by your stepfather? *Terrible!*" A thirteen-year-old makes a list of the five funerals of friends he's been to this year. A twelve-year-old tells about guns in his tree house. Side by side, I sit with the children and type out their words as they are speaking. They are flabbergasted that somebody finds their words so fascinating that she is typing out their stories. But what am I listening to? I am listening to the whisper of the death of America's childhood.

From my teachers at Weihsien I learned about the necessity for structure, for comforting predictability, in creating a safe world for children. Today, at the Youth Center, policemen who have known our children on the streets as ruffians and incorrigibles and killers have come in and seen them quietly doing their schoolwork, not speaking until they have raised their hands for permission, not getting out of their seats, walking in a straight and orderly line, paying attention and doing what they're told, and they just shake their heads in disbelief. "How is this possible?" they ask. And I say, "You make a safe feeling by creating a comfortingly predictable world." It was the same thing my teachers did in that concentration camp. Every day, the child knows that the structure will not vary, that they will do exactly what they did the day before and the day after tomorrow. They are constantly reminded: This is when you get up. This is when you scrub. This is when you have a morning meeting. This is when you line up for school. For children who have known little except chaos all through their young lives, this kind of structure can be lifesaving, soul-saving. Because it comes from love.

When the war ended, we eased into America by settling in a small town in Michigan. Spring Arbor embodied the humble, simple way of life, with small-town values and a small-town pace, that my parents were looking for. But conditions there were almost as primitive as those in China. The only house available had no running water, a pump in the sink, and an outhouse in the tiny backyard. That first winter, my mother got frostbite from washing clothes in cold water. But the house was near a church, and also near a small Christian college where my mother had taught before the war. My parents continued their religious work, which is what they were doing when the sawmill accident happened. All I worried about, in the midst of my terror, was would any boy ever want to date a girl without a hand? Would I be a freak? Would I be able to play volleyball? And my dad said "I don't know why not."

That year, I was assigned to do a research paper in school. My father suggested a topic: "How about *handicaps*?" We searched out stories about people who were handicapped. Helen Keller, the deaf, dumb, and blind child who astonished the world. Franklin Roosevelt, who inspired America from a wheel-chair. My father told me that handicaps are what are on the *inside*. When my father put those words inside me—"I don't see why not"—he made another picture in my mind—a picture of a girl who *could*. He planted that image inside me and made it grow. People do not see me as a woman with one hand; nor do I see myself as handicapped. I just firmly believe that a parent or a grown-up can turn a child's inner vision around by pouring in a different picture. That's what I try to do with the children I work with now.

When we were growing up, there were three things a woman could aspire to be: a nurse, a secretary, or a teacher. My mother thought I would probably end up being a preacher's wife, but I ended up becoming a teacher, like many of my childhood girlfriends. One of my first jobs was at an inner-city high school in New Jersey. I loved it, instantly. I was the crazy teacher in the bleachers who threw her coat in the air and carried on every time Camden High's football team scored a touchdown. I took my entire English class to the state champion-ships, where they stood up in the middle of the bleachers and yelled out lines from *Macbeth*: "Tomorrow, and tomorrow, and tomorrow . . ." I always had a tumble of journalism students in my living room and kitchen, with Coca-Cola cans and pizza all over the carpet, putting out the student newspaper. Last year, a student I once had—a not very gifted student, if the truth be told—came with his girlfriend, who had come to see me. He said, "Mary Previte! There can only be one Mary Previte." And there on the carpet in my office, he quoted the entire *Macbeth* soliloquy: "Tomorrow, and tomorrow, and tomorrow/Creeps in this petty pace from day to day . . ." His girlfriend looked at him in absolute astonishment. She said, "I cannot believe my ears. After thirty-five years, how did you remember all that?"

"Footprints That Last Forever": That's the title of one of the most important stories I tell the kids. It begins when I was a young teacher at my first teaching job at Camden High School. I was a small person, and didn't look like a teacher, and in my homeroom there was a kid named Lewis Katz—a bright, irrepressible boy who could have become either a high achiever or a troublemaker. Did I know that anybody in my homeroom was watching this teacher who was so young that everybody thought she was one of the students? Did I know that out of that huge school of 2,100 kids, a young boy would remember his homeroom teacher when he needed to find somebody to change this place around? "Don't ever forget," I tell the kids, "that whoever you are, wherever you go, whoever you might happen to meet, you leave footprints that last forever."

I taught for five years before taking a leave of absence when I became pregnant. By this time, I had married a college classmate, a minister's son, whose parents had known my parents. For twelve years, I stayed home and became a suburban matron, got elected to the school board, taught Sunday school, and did volunteer work for the League of Women Voters. By the time my daughter was in junior high, just as I was beginning to tire of what I called my "crabgrass and diaper-rash years," there was suddenly an explosion that brought me to the Youth Center twenty years ago.

My former homeroom student Lewis Katz had just been elected to political office; the Camden County Youth Center was part of his department. At that time, the center was a snake pit. Politicians called it "Something out of *Oliver Twist*." There were frequent riots, at least one a week. Kids were injured, teachers were injured, kids were punched, locked up, there were long, long days and weeks of solitary confinement. Human excrement in the basement. Plaster exploding off the walls and ceilings with mildew and rust. The first weekend after being appointed superintendent of the center, I received a phone call at home: "There's a riot in progress. It's serious, you'd better come." I was dressed in a flowing red, white, and blue hostess gown, just about to welcome my guests to a dinner party. Crystal and china and candlelight, the beef bourguignon simmering on the stove. I rushed out, pulled into the parking lot . . . I can still hear the tom-tom beat of the riot going on inside. The correctional officers were standing by and gleefully waiting to see how this nice housewife from suburbia, a political appointee, was planning to put down a riot. Upstairs, the whole building was shaking. The boys were cursing and spitting and banging and battering and kicking, bruising their fists against the locked doors—the noise just shook me to the core. The officers were armed with riot gear and Mace, trying to smash kids against the wall with mattresses. I went up to the first door and started whispering: "Stevie, tell me what is going on." Up and down the hall, all the boys stopped battering and screaming, straining to hear if this boy would rat on them. Then they started asking me questions: Why was I dressed in that gown? How much did it cost? What was I eating at my party? How old was my daughter? Pretty normal kiddish-type questions. So it was the boys themselves who calmed the riot, hooked by their curiosity about this lady standing there in a hostess dress, talking quietly to them at each door.

Almost overnight, there were dramatic changes. The riots stopped immediately. My budget the first year was fifty cents per kid per year—you couldn't buy crayons for that. The two activities at the center were buffing floors and watching television. There was no school, no possibility of learning going on. Kids in deep trouble, lost kids, were hidden out of sight in a snake-pit campus, so you didn't have to see them or hear them or remember that they were society's failures. We instituted programs that tested them, motivated them, helped them succeed. We added tutoring and created rewards for following the rules. When we applied to the federal government for money to build a new building, the federal investigator said, "This program tops anything anywhere in the nation." Within three years, we had our new building.

I always felt I was just an ordinary American, but now I find that I have an extraordinary perspective because of where I've been. All people who have lived long have that unique perspective, based on the cumulative experience of their lives. Instead of saying, as I might have once, "Oh no, why me, why can't somebody else do it?" I now see that there *is* nobody else who knows exactly what I know, who has exactly what I have to give. I feel now that all the disparate elements of my life have brought me to an understanding of what I'm supposed to do—to bring the news to people who have the power to change conditions for children by giving those children a voice, giving the voiceless a voice. I try to be a public-address system for the voices of the children, pained, anguished, crying out for help. Now I know now why I was in a concentration camp, why I was separated from my family for five years, why I lost my hand. Because all those losses made me more sensitive, more effective, and more profoundly connected to other human beings.

When Tina, one of our most troubled girls, walks down the hallway holding my handless arm as a gesture of love, I know that it's a way of helping me get closer to kids who have also lost so much, far more than just a hand. They have lost their souls, their reason to live. What's the loss of a hand compared to that? The times I can make an instant connection are when I talk about how I lost my hand. Opening up and revealing the innermost secrets that other people might want to hide gives them a chance to do the very same thing.

I often speak to children's advocate groups all across the country, and one of my favorite speeches is called "You Can Change the Shape of Your Mountain." It goes like this:

> *A young traveler on a mountainside in the Alps was puzzled as he looked in the distance at what appeared to be an old shepherd among puny sheep and goats. And as he watched, the gnarled old hand of the shepherd would reach into a bucket draped across his arm and pluck something out. Then the old man would pierce the mountainside with his shepherd's crook and drop something gently into the ground, and tap it softly with his foot.*
>
> *The young traveler approached the old shepherd and asked, "Old man, what is it you are doing here on this godforsaken mountain?" And the old man looked up, as though surely the youth should know, and said, "I am changing the shape of my mountain."*
>
> *The young man laughed, because everybody knows you cannot change the shape of a mountain. But he drew up close to watch. And the gnarled old hand reached into the bucket draped across his arm and plucked out another acorn. And then with his shepherd's crook, he pierced the mountainside and dropped it gently into the ground.*
>
> *Again the young man asked, "Old man, what is it you are doing on this mountainside?" The shepherd gave the same reply: "I am changing the shape of my mountain." And the young man walked sadly away, because everybody knows you cannot change the shape of a mountain.*
>
> *And then the young man himself grew old, and dreamed of retracing the steps of his youth. The map he had brought told him that he had reached the mountain, and yet nothing he*

saw seemed the same. Where once there had been a godforsaken hillside, there were now giant oak trees, and country villages nestled in the shade of their massive branches, and children running down country pathways, and clouds drifting slowly overhead. And then the traveler remembered the old man who had said he could change the shape of his mountain.

Yes, we can change our world, but only one tiny acorn at a time, one child at a time. There is power in each of us to change the shape of the world. And we need to find out what our mountain is, and start working on changing it.

My mother-in-law was a minister's wife who chose to stay home and not work in the work-for-pay world. Whatever she did, she did with grace and loveliness. On summer evenings, there would be a tangle of kids on her front porch, with the smell of her homemade pizza wafting through the summer night. Her unique contribution was to make the world a lovelier place. The world of the children I work with would be enhanced by such a person. Who is to say that working for a paycheck is more important than Mama Previte's work with the little kids on the block?

The Bible tells the story of Moses out in the desert. God says, "Moses, what's that you've got in your hand?" Moses replies, "My shepherd's crook." And God says, "Well, I'm going to use you and that shepherd's crook to liberate an entire people." Many chapters later, here's David, the shepherd boy: "Hey, David, what is that you've got in your hand?" David says, "I've got a pebble—five smooth stones that I found in the brook." God says, "Use them to kill the giant Goliath." And David used them in a slingshot and the Philistines were defeated.

What do *you* have in your hand? Grandma Previte had the touch of generosity in her hand—the cookies, the china cup, the flower just picked from the garden, the joy she gave to other people with the tenderness in her heart. She was a tiny glint of loveliness in an increasingly ugly world. So I say, each of us holds something exceptional in our hand, a magnificent gift just waiting to be given away. What I hold in my hand is not more important than what you have in yours. Use that gift. Give it to a child, any child. All children need a caring older person to go into their schools, touch them, be in their class. . . . You may be the person to shape a kid's life—the one person who is so enamored with that child that that love, that belief, will turn his life around. Who knows how long such footprints you leave might last? They might even last forever.